ALFA ROMEO

an illustrated history

Originally published as *Alfa Romeo Anniversario* by HEEL Verlag, GmbH,
Königswinter, Germany ©2020
Translated from the German by David Johnston

Library of Congress Control Number: 2023941046

Content collection: Sascha Wolfinger (Publisher)
Editor: Christian Schön
Cover design by Chris Bower
Production design by Danielle D. Farmer
Type set in DraftD/DIN

ISBN: 978-0-7643-6730-4
Printed in China

Published by Schiffer Publishing, Ltd.
4880 Lower Valley Road
Atglen, PA 19310
Phone: (610) 593-1777; Fax: (610) 593-2002
Email: Info@schifferbooks.com
Web: www.schifferbooks.com

MIX
Paper from responsible sources
FSC® C167893

ALFA ROMEO

an illustrated history

1910–2020

SCHIFFER PUBLISHING
4880 Lower Valley Road • Atglen, PA 19310

K62156 TO

110 years after the founding of the company, the Alfa Romeo Giulia is representative of the brand's great history. Like its predecessors from the 1960s, the current model shines with a uniquely Italian style.

CONTENTS

14

56

86

102

158

198

Dear friends of Alfa Romeo,

There are not many automobile brands that can look back on a tradition that spans 110 years. When the first Tipo 24HP rolled out of a small production hall in Milan's Portello district in 1910, none of those present could have imagined what an icon Alfa Romeo would one day become.

After all, technologically the 24HP was already setting standards. With the ability to reach 62 mph (100 kph), it was far ahead of its time. The 24HP was thus the nucleus of an innovative spirit that has always characterized Alfa Romeo. This spirit of innovation has been driven by the engineers' enthusiasm for the search for something even better, even more powerful—a spirit of innovation that, combined with unmistakable Italian design, has produced some of the most fascinating automobiles of all time. We call it "the Mechanics of Emotions," the values of technology and emotions that for us are inseparable.

These emotions have always been passed on to the most creative designers of their respective eras. Great names such as Bertone, Pininfarina, Zagato, and Touring have had a decisive influence on the automotive designs of entire eras with concept cars based on Alfa Romeo models. Studies such as the so-called BAT-Mobiles from the 1950s or the extremely futuristic Tipo-33 variations from the 1960s have virtually become the epitome of the show car.

Beyond the often-radical concept cars, the company's unerring sense of timeless elegance and unique style ensure that Alfa Romeo automobiles regularly rank among the winners of the world's most important design competitions. This was already the case in 1947, when an Alfa Romeo 6C 2500 won the *Concorso d'Eleganza* at the Villa d'Este on Lake Como, which is still a leading automotive event in the twenty-first century. And it is still the case today, when Alfa Romeo's current models are chosen as winners in reader surveys conducted by major international magazines or in important industrial design competitions.

In addition to its unmistakable design, Alfa Romeo's fascination is due in no small part to its success in motorsports. Five world championship titles, including two in Formula 1, a dozen European championships, eleven victories in the legendary *Mille Miglia* endurance race, and victory in the German Touring Car Championship (DTM) against the strong domestic brands, are just the tip of the iceberg. Alfa Romeo also has its own team in the current Formula 1 World Championship. The cars proudly bear the legend "Racing since 1910."

From the very beginning, racing has been an ideal test laboratory for Alfa Romeo's innovative technologies, which subsequently led to even sportier performance in production vehicles. This was the case with overhead camshafts, which were used by Alfa Romeo as early as 1914, and extends to the famous TwinSpark dual ignition system and carbon fiber body components, which today ensure low weight in the Alfa Romeo Giulia and Stelvio.

And so, in every Alfa Romeo that drives on the road there beats the *Cuore Sportivo* (sporting heart) of a racing car. It is this sporting heart and expertise from motorsport that make every drive in an Alfa Romeo a very special experience. This is not limited to the lap records on the Nordschleife of the Nürburgring that our test drivers set with the Giulia and Stelvio.

The *Quadrifoglio* (four-leaf clover) is a symbol of the direct influence of the knowledge gained from motorsport on Alfa Romeo's production cars. First used in 1923 as a good luck charm for the *Targa Florio* road race, the four-leaf clover today represents the pinnacle of performance capability at Alfa Romeo. With 510 hp (375 kW), the Alfa Romeo *Giulia Quadrifoglio* and Alfa Romeo *Stelvio Quadrifoglio* are the most powerful production cars in the history of the brand. These are surpassed only by the Alfa Romeo Giulia GTA and Alfa Romeo Giulia GTAm limited-edition models, which, with an engine output of 540 hp (397 kW), bring pure motorsport technology to the road.

The fascination and innovative power of Alfa Romeo, which has remained unbroken for 110 years, are very much also a credit to the passion and commitment of the people behind the company. Their pioneering spirit and great ideas have helped our brand influence the evolution of the automobile as a whole for more than a century.

Alongside the most important vehicles from 110 years and the greatest successes in international motorsport, *Alfa Romeo: An Illustrated History* also precisely recalls these people. With this scope, the book takes you on an exciting journey through the great history of Alfa Romeo. I hope you enjoy reading this book.

Yours,
Niccolò Biagioli
Brand Country Manager, Alfa Romeo & Jeep®

110 YEARS IN TIME LAPSE

1910

Founding of the *Anonima Lombarda Fabbrica Automobili* (Lombardy Automobile Manufacturing Company, or A.L.F.A.). Production of the *Tipo 24HP* began in a factory in Milan's Portello district. The model was also used in racing.

1923

Ugo Sivocci wins the Targa Florio driving the *Tipo RL*. His good luck charm is a four-leaf clover, the *Quadrifoglio Verde*.

1928

The *Tipo 6C 1500* wins Alfa Romeo's first victory in the *Mille Miglia*.

1935

The Alfa Romeo 8C 2900A was one of the most impressive and technically advanced automobiles of the prewar era.

1915

Nicola Romeo acquired the majority of shares in A.L.F.A. and in 1920 renamed the company Alfa Romeo.

1925

With the *Tipo P2*, Alfa Romeo wins the first world championship in the history of the automobile.

1931

The *Tipo 8C 2300* wins the 24-hour race at Le Mans. Three more victories followed by 1934.

1949

A Tipo 6C 2500 with a body by Touring wins the *Concours d'Elegance* at the Villa d'Este. This model was subsequently produced in small numbers under this name and purchased by various celebrities.

1967

Alfa Romeo was the only European automaker to display a concept car at the World's Fair in Montreal (Canada) in 1967. It subsequently went into production as the *Montreal*.

1951

Alfa Romeo defends its Formula 1 title with the *Tipo 159*. Juan Manuel Fangio becomes the world champion driver.

1954

With the *Giulia*, Alfa Romeo succeeds in breaking into the European market.

1962

Alfa Romeo enters the small car sector for the first time with the *Giuletta*. This model heralds the change from a manufactory to a mass producer.

1949 1950 1951 1953 1954 1962 1963 1965 1967

1950

With the *Tipo 158*, Alfa Romeo wins the Formula 1 world championship, newly introduced that year. Giuseppe "Nino" Farina becomes world driving champion.

1953

In this and the following two years, the three *Berlinetta Aerodinamica Technica* (B.A.T. for short) concept cars designed by Bertone's chief designer Franco Scaglione attract a great deal of attention.

1963

Opening of the Arese factory.

1965

Unveiling of the Alfa Romeo *Giulia GTA* with light-metal body. The racing version won several brand and driver titles in the European Touring Car Championship.

1968

Half a dozen concept cars were built on the basis of the Alfa Romeo *Tipo 33 Stradale* and went on to influence automobile design for the next few years. Among these concept cars was the *Carabo*, produced by the Carrozzeria Bertone.

1983

Unveiling of the Alfa Romeo 33, of which almost a million are sold during its production life of twelve years.

1993

Alfa Romeo wins the German Touring Car Championship (DTM). The Italian Nicola Larini becomes driving champion in the 155 V6 TI.

1975

Alfa Romeo won the World Championship of Makes with the *Tipo 33TT12*. In 1977 it added another title in the world championship of long-distance racing.

1985

The Alfa Romeo 75 is unveiled on the company's seventy-fifth birthday.

1997

Alfa Romeo unveils the Model 156. Walter de Silva incorporated features of some of the brand's legendary vehicles in its design.

1972

The *Alfasud* was the brand's first production vehicle with front-wheel drive. A new factory was built to produce the car at Pomigliano d'Arco near Naples.

The new mid-class model was given the tradition-rich name *Alfetta*.

1977

Unveiling of the Alfa Romeo *Giulietta*.

FCA
FIAT CHRYSLER AUTOMOBILES

1986

Alfa Romeo becomes part of Fiat (later Fiat Chrysler Automobiles and today part of Stellantis N.V.).

1989

Designed in conjunction with Zagato, the Alfa Romeo SZ (Coupé) and RZ (Spider, from 1992) sports cars make headlines.

2005

Unveiling of the Alfa Romeo 159 sedan, which the magazine *AutoBild* selects as the "Most Beautiful Car in the World" in its class.

2006

Just 500 examples of the *8C Competizione* eight-cylinder sports car are built.

2010

The Alfa Romeo *Giulietta* arrives on the market on Alfa Romeo's 100th birthday. The top model, the 375hp *Quadrifoglio*, sets sedan lap records on the Nürburgring-Nordschleife.

2013

The Alfa Romeo 4C establishes a lap record for its segment on the Nurburgring's Nordschleife.

2015

Unveiling of the new generation of models.

2016

Alfa Romeo unveils the *Stelvio* at the Los Angeles Auto Show. The brand's first SUV wins numerous design awards.

2018

Alfa Romeo makes its return to Formula 1 together with the Swiss team Sauber.

2019

Unveiled at the Geneva Salon, the *Tonale* concept SUV is the brand's first hybrid vehicle.

2020

The 540-hp Alfa Romeo *Giulia GTAm* is the most powerful production automobile in the brand's history.

THE ALFA ROMEO MYTH–
A LEGEND IS BORN

Over the past 110 years, Alfa Romeo has built some of the most beautiful cars of all time—often in teamwork with outside body makers.

WIN ON SUNDAY, SELL ON MONDAY

In the 1950s, the will to win in motorsport was responsible for some of the most beautiful Alfa Romeos of all time.

metal. There was a reason for this change: the standard *Giulietta Sprint Speciale* model offered by Alfa Romeo could not hold its own on the racetrack against the version from an external body maker—the *Giulietta Sprint Zagato*.

With its aerodynamically sophisticated but rather long body, the *Giulietta Sprint Speciale* was fast on the straights but not nimble enough in the corners. And this is precisely where Zagato came in. He covered the *Giulietta Sprint*'s chassis with bodywork that fit as closely as possible, of course also struck from aluminum. With an identical wheelbase, the *Giulietta Sprint Zagato* was more than 3.28 feet (1 meter) shorter than the Giulietta Sprint Speciale. It also weighed around 154 pounds (70 kg) less.

Alfa Romeo resolved the burgeoning conflict between the Bertone and Zagato design studios with an ingenious compromise. Zagato concentrated on racing, eventually developing a second variant of the *Giulietta SZ* with a longer rear end (*coda tronca*). The *Giulietta Sprint Speciale*, on the other hand, was now built largely of steel—at Bertone—in the interests of lower production costs and was equipped with a more comfortable interior. This turned the racing car into a *Gran Turismo* for fast business trips.

From 1963, the *Giulia*'s 112 hp, 1.6-liter four-cylinder engine provided even better performance, while at the same time the car underwent a name change. The *Giulia Sprint Speciale* was not intended for racing use anyway. Alfa Romeo had long had another arrow in its quiver for that.

The Alfa Romeo *Tipo 33 Stradale*, which was just under 40 inches (1 meter) high, brought motorsport technology to the road. The eight-cylinder engine produced 230 hp and revved to just under 9,000 rpm. Only twelve were built.

IN SHORT

Alfa Romeo Giulia GT Sprint—this name was too long for the fans. They simply called the coupe the Bertone, after the Bertone Design Studio.

The production version of the "*Bertone*" (*previous two-page spread*) was a beloved street sportscar, while the GTA version with aluminum body (*right*), of which just 500 were made, served as a basis for racecars.

It's rather unusual for the developer's name to appear in the name of the finished model. Even more unusual is a car known almost exclusively under the name of its designer. Perhaps the most prominent example of this is the "Bertone." Well, this designation was not really official. But for German fans, Alfa Romeo Giulia GT Sprint was just too long. Without further ado, they named the coupe of the series after the body maker, which was responsible for the car's iconic shape.

This is certainly also due to the fact that the *Giulia GT Sprint* is a so-called century design. The "Bertone" undoubtedly brought the Alfa Romeo brand back to the attention of car lovers outside Italy in the mid-1960s. The agile coupe became the dream car of countless young sports car lovers.

To be fair, it should be mentioned that it was not the company owner Giuseppe "Nuccio" Bertone himself but the young Giorgio Giugiaro who played a leading role in the development of the design. This was long before he made a name for himself with his own studio and further century designs.

There is more behind the "Bertone" than just a sheet-metal symbol of timelessness, however. The 2+2 seat coupe is one of the first examples of a successful platform strategy that is now the industry standard. The Alfa Romeo *Giulia* was available as a sedan, coupe, convertible, and station wagon. All variants shared identical technology, the so-called platform.

It was the sedan that launched the series. In 1962, the first model established the league of sports sedans. The 113hp *TI Super* version—TI the acronym for the *Turismo Internazionale* motorsport category, of which just 501 were built—offered driving performance that until then had been achieved only by sports cars.

But the light-alloy four-cylinder engine with twin camshafts, which has long since become a legend, was not the *Giulia*'s only strength. Engineer Orazio Satta Puliga applied the experience gained in aircraft construction to give the body smooth surfaces with precisely calculated edges and beads.

What fans now call a "bone tail" is actually a Kamm tail, named after German aerodynamics pioneer Wunibald Kamm. The result was a drag coefficient of 0.34—a record value for a four-door sedan.

The model range was rapidly expanded. Puliga first commissioned Studio Bertone, by then already a trusted partner of Alfa Romeo, to design a coupe. It was based on the chassis of the sedan, which was shortened by 6.3 inches (16 cm).

For the body, Giugiaro skillfully developed the shape of the *Giulietta Sprint*. The edge hood, which takes its name

Authorities and road services also appreciated the sportiness of the Alfa Romeo *Giulia*. They could order a station wagon version from the Carrozzeria Giorgetti, among others.

ALFA ROMEO LEFT PRODUCTION OF STATION WAGON VERSIONS OF THE GIULIA TO EXTERNAL BODY MAKERS.

from a visible shoulder between the hood and the front end panel, became the trademark of the first series produced from 1963.

And because the *Giulia GT Sprint* was also to make a career on the racetrack, Alfa Romeo's racing department Autodelta replaced the steel body with an almost identical version made of lightweight aluminum. Its distinctive features included visible rivets, for example, on the roof.

Weight was also saved elsewhere, with smaller door handles and a fancy wooden steering wheel with perforated spokes, ultimately more than 220 pounds (100 kg) compared to the standard model. In addition, engine output was increased to 115 hp, among other things with dual ignition.

The *Gran Turismo Alleggerita* or, in short, the GTA, is no longer available. Only 500 of each of the two variants of the Giulia GTA, with 97.6- and 79.3-cubic inch (1600 and 1300cc) engines, respectively, were built, all of them handmade at Autodelta.

Alfa Romeo would never offer the *Giulia* as a station wagon from the factory. Such a step would probably have gone too far for the sports car maker at that point. But because the *carabinieri* (the national gendarmerie of Italy), for example, appreciated the *Giulia*'s superior performance in the fight against evil, various coachbuilders stepped into the breach. Among others, the Carrozzerias Colli and Giorgetti fitted a total of 800 sedans with station wagon bodies, with and without side windows. They bore the name affixes *Promiscua*, *Giardinetta*, and *Familiare*.

The situation was different for the convertible. Alfa Romeo drew on the expertise of a design studio that had also been a trusted partner for decades. Milan's Carrozzeria Touring received semi-finished coupes from the Arese plant, exclusively with 97.6-cubic-inch (1600 cc) engines, and replaced the steel roof with a fabric top. Apart from that, Touring did not touch Giorgio Giugiaro's original design. The "Bertone" was also perfect as a convertible.

Previous spread: Under the sign of the Z. The letter logo on the front fender reveals that the Alfa Romeo *Giulia TZ* was designed by Zagato. Beneath the aluminum body was a tubular frame (Italian: *tubolare*).

Anatomy of a sports car with a touch of luxury—the "*Bertone*" (the GTV 1750 variant in the photo above) was the perfect everyday car.

The Alfa Romeo *Giulia* (*on the right*), a version with a 97.6-cubic-inch engine) was one of the first autos developed in a wind tunnel.

The radiator grille of a modern Alfa Romeo is shaped like a shield. Along the way, this iconic design feature has undergone many changes.

THE EVOLUTION OF THE *SCUDETTO* ("LITTLE SHIELD")

1927

6C 1500
At this time, Alfa Romeo primarily built chassis, which were outfitted with bodies by various body makers. The radiator is typical for the six-cylinder sports car.

1931

8C 2300 Monza
The Grand Prix version of the Tipo 8C 2300 was given a rounded radiator housing for aerodynamic reasons. The longitudinal openings parallel to the radiator openings were introduced to deliver more air to the eight-cylinder engine.

1937

8C 2900 B
The radiator was no longer exposed to the slipstream, instead being housed within the streamlined Superleggara body. The 8C 2900 was the first to have a heart-shaped radiator grille. It was again flanked by longitudinal openings.

1939

6C 2500 SS Corsa
This race car had an interpretation of the rounded radiator opening with the characteristic longitudinal holes in the upper part of the radiator grille. The location of the headlights–no longer between the fenders and the radiator, but almost on the outer sides–was new.

1947

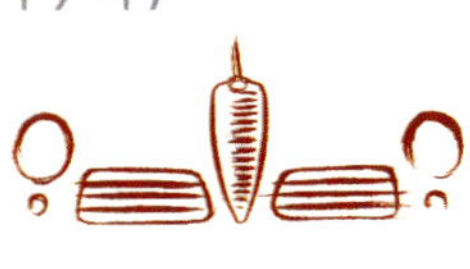

6C 2500 Sport Freccia d´Oro
The heart- or shield-shaped grille became a stylistic device. The cooling air flowed through openings on the sides into the engine bay.

1949

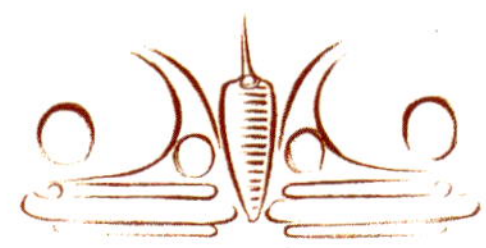

6C 2500 Super Sport Villa d´Este
Ribs gave the *scudetto* the look of a shield. The cooling air openings on the sides were concealed by the two halves of the bumper. The main headlights were augmented by centrally positioned secondary headlights.

1950

1900
Characteristic features are the scudetto, which is reduced in height, and the *baffi* (Italian for mustaches), which extend to the sides and move close to the headlights.

1952

1900 C52 Disco Volante
The front of the flat sports car has the typical Alfa Romeo characteristics. However, due to its lenticular cross-section body, the *baffi* (mustaches) seem to push the headlights upward.

1955

Giulietta Berlina
The small size and narrowness of this sedan gave the front of the vehicle a somewhat squarer appearance, which is now finally shaped as a three-part element consisting of the radiator grille and "mustaches."

1955

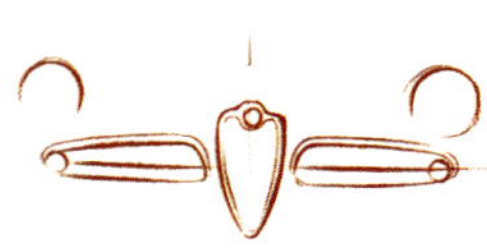

Giulietta Spider
The front of the roadster is flatter than that of the sedan, but the typical scudetto with the prominent ribs remains.

1957

Giulietta Sprint Speciale
The focus is on the aerodynamics of the coupe, which was originally developed for competition use. The cooling air opening is also secondary to aerodynamics. For the first time, it is designed as a single opening, which is given the look typical of the brand by means of a scudetto attached as a decorative element.

1962

Giulia Sprint
The "mustaches" are now covered by a flat grille.

1962

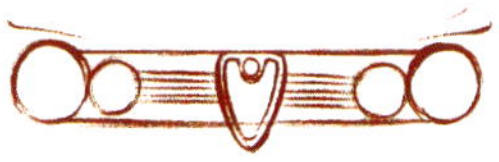

Giulia
Cooling air openings now extend over the entire width of the vehicle, and the headlights are integrated into the front. The centrally placed heart shares the grille.

1963

Giulia Sprint GT
The headlights, moved back to the center, and the heart dividing the radiator grille provide the typical look. The GTA versions intended for racing can be recognized by the two additional elongated holes on the sides below the scudetto.

1968

Giulia Sprint GT Veloce
With the introduction of the 2-liter engine, the coupe received a new radiator grille, and the scudetto was not part of this grille. Thus, for the first time, it served merely as an ornament.

1972

Alfetta 1800
The no-frills shape is typical of the 1970s. The heart again rests on the body.

1977

Giulietta
The horizontal grille with large rectangular headlights, the laterally positioned turn signal lights, and the central screwed-on scudetto are clearly structured. The row of elongated holes of different sizes underneath is a sporty stylistic element.

1980

Alfetta GTV6
The grille-mounted scudetto of the Alfetta GT underwent a far-reaching model update in the top model of the series; it was stylized and made part of the plastic grille.

1985

75
Characteristic is the return of the "mustaches," formed by the tunnel-shaped radiator grille and the scudetto placed slightly above it.

1987

164
The scudetto became part of the hood.

1994

145
The scudetto is strongly accentuated by the lines of the hood. The plastic insert at the lower end of the hood divides the radiator grille above the bumper into two small "mustaches."

1996

Nuvola
The study anticipated design elements of the 159 series. The scudetto was more accentuated, the "mustaches" enjoyed a renaissance, and the headlights were positioned higher.

1997

156
The multiple-award-winning sedan was adorned with a shiny chrome scudetto, accentuated by the lines in the bumper and hood. The elongated holes placed in the lower half were reminiscent of the 8C 2300

2000

147
The front of the car has classic features that show kinship with the Giulietta family or the 6C 2500 Villa d'Este.

2016

Giulia
With the Alfa Romeo Giulia, the central air intake becomes more dominant, a nod to its powerful engines. Bi-Xenon technology allows for narrower headlights.

CONVERTIBLES

In the first half of the twentieth century, cars often lacked a roof. When at some point sedans become the standard, Alfa Romeo continued the tradition of the sporty roadster, called a spider in Italian.

CONVERTIBLES

In the first half of the twentieth century, cars often lacked a roof. When at some point sedans become the standard, Alfa Romeo continued the tradition of the sporty roadster, called a spider in Italian.

From the first (*previous spread*) to the second generation (*right*), the Alfa Romeo Spider became more angular. This model's nickname was *coda tronca* (truncated tail).

ALFA ROMEO PRODUCED THIS SPIDER SERIES OVER FOUR MODEL GENERATIONS WITH ONLY A FEW CHANGES.

The motion picture was a breakthrough for two talents of the century. In *The Graduate*, Dustin Hoffman played the internally torn Benjamin Braddock so convincingly that his rise to Hollywood icon status was preordained. And Braddock's Alfa Romeo Spider fit so well into the Californian high society of the 1960s that it burned itself into the collective memory of movie fans as one of the most important movie cars in history.

Admittedly, Alfa Romeo's tradition of open sports cars goes back well into the early days of the last century. As early as the 1930s, there were convertibles with bodies by Ghia, Zagato, Touring, and also Pininfarina. But these models were built only in small numbers and were exclusive luxury cars. In 1955, the *Giulietta Spider*, and from 1962 the *Giulia Spider*, were more down to earth.

However, the roadster experience really took off with the 1966 Alfa Romeo Spider, whose body shape–as with the open-top versions of the *Giulietta* and *Giulia*–was the work of design legend Battista "Pinin" Farina. It was his last work, since Farina died shortly after the car's world premiere at the Geneva Motor Show in March 1966. With the new, slightly larger platform–from the *Giulia* instead of the *Giulietta*–the master craftsman took a completely new approach. He gave the new Spider curved lines; from the side, the windshield, enclosed by a thin frame, and the small triangular windows were barely noticeable.

The wide bead running along the entire flank of the automobile was a striking feature. Like the Plexiglas headlight covers, this had an aerodynamic function but also added rigidity to the sheet metal surfaces of the doors and fenders.

The world premiere of the Alfa Romeo Spider took place on the luxury liner Raffaello during a voyage from Genoa to New York.

Introduced by Alfa Romeo in 1955, the Giulietta Spider made the Italian roadster socially acceptable. The model was inspired by the American importer Max Hoffman.

At the rear, too, the Alfa Romeo Spider ran out flat and in a semicircle. The unique design, which today is known to every *Alfista* as the "round tail," divides the fan community. Many purists find the design too feminine. The nickname "*Osso di Sepia*" also made the rounds. Although this sounds like an Italian declaration of love, it translates rather unflatteringly as "cuttlefish bone," which is a birdcage accessory.

The model name *Duetto* was chosen by the public; however, it couldn't be officially adopted due to trademark issues. Ironically, it's precisely these two designations that made the 1966 Spider unmistakable in the subsequent series of Spider generations.

With the 1970 model year, the studio now called Pininfarina modernized the Spider. The biggest change was its straight-cut rear end; the "*Osso di Sepia*" became the somewhat shorter "Fastback" (*coda tronca* in Italian). The front was modified in a barely visible way. The badge was lower and slightly wider, and the bumper was still split, but the two halves were now one-piece components. In addition, the windshield had a flatter rake.

As with the preceding model, the body was manufactured by Pininfarina in Grugliasco, with the technology subsequently added at the neighboring Arese plant. The Fastback generation, which was built for just under fifteen years, was discontinued in 1982.

Spoilers were in vogue in the mid-1980s, and even the third-generation Alfa Romeo Spider couldn't do without them. Again at Pininfarina, completely redesigned front and rear bumpers were created using insights from aerodynamics–and with little regard for style. The rear spoiler, the rear bumper (which extended to the wheel wells), and the sweeping front spoiler beneath the flat front end were controversial. The classic Alfa Romeo badge was replaced by a triangular injection-molded piece emblazoned with a significantly larger crest at its center. Alfa Romeo marketed this model generation of the Spider as the *Aerodinamica*.

Fiat, Alfa Romeo's new owner from 1986, had long-term plans for the Spider, but the development of a completely new model would still take a few years. As a temporary solution, Pininfarina was given the task of redesigning the classic. The result, at least today, is worlds better than the "rubber lip" of the third model generation.

Exquisite pedigree—from the "*Osso di Sepia*" of 1966, the family of roadsters offered under the model name Alfa Romeo Spider extended to the 939 series, built between 2006 and 2010. This German-language advertisement has the heading "A picture of a legend: the new Alfa Spider."

BEAUTIFUL REAR END

With the 159 and 156 models, Alfa Romeo brought not only Italian style to the sedan segment. As Sportwagons, both models also redefine the term “lifestyle station wagon.”

At times, more station wagon versions of the Alfa Romeo 159 (*previous spread*) and Alfa Romeo 156 (*right*) were sold than sedans.

Fans and the trade public fell at the feet of the Alfa Romeo 156 at the Frankfurt IAA in the fall of 1997. And indeed, the four-door sedan returned the brand to its former glory. It went on to win numerous design awards and the readers' polls in the major automotive magazines. An international jury of journalists named the Alfa Romeo 156 "Car of the Year 1998."

Designer Walter de Silva, at that time head of the in-house *Centro Stile*, created a monument to himself with the Alfa Romeo 156. It invoked–in some places strikingly, in others subtly–the design of classic Alfa Romeo models. The eye was immediately drawn to the pronounced Alfa Romeo badge, which extended into the bumper and necessitated the sideways placement of the license plate–another historical invocation. The visual highlight, however, was the handles for the rear doors integrated into the C-pillar. They lent coupe-like features to the silhouette of the Alfa Romeo 156.

The new model, which was built at Pomigliano d'Arco near Naples in one of Europe's most modern automobile plants, gave Alfa Romeo a strong image boost. The station wagon version, officially called the "*Sportwagon*," also played a major role. Alfa Romeo pursued the lifestyle station wagon strategy even more consistently than other brands. The Alfa Romeo 156 *Crosswagon Q4*, a variant with four-wheel drive and some off-road details, and the Alfa Romeo 156 *GTA Sportwagon* were the icing on the cake.

The three letters GTA paid homage to the successful racing cars of the 1960s and 1970s. At the heart of the sedan and station wagon in GTA guise was a V-6 engine with an output of 250 hp, up to that point the most powerful production engine in the history of the brand. Because both models were pushing into new speed ranges, they were given body details optimized from an aerodynamic point of view.

As highly praised as the design of the Alfa Romeo 156 was in its presentation year of 1997, after five years it was time for a facelift. Andreas Zapatinas, the new head of *Centro Stile Alfa Romeo*, shaped the front end much more aggressively. The triple headlights placed behind clear glass had almost a predatory look. The scudetto became even more striking.

By the time production of the Alfa Romeo 156 ended in 2005, it had almost single-handedly saved the brand. A

Iconic design—in designing the Alfa Romeo 156, Walter de Silva (*photo at bottom of previous page*) invoked legendary vehicles from the brand's history.

The second generation of the Alfa Romeo 156 (*top right*) received a redesigned front end. The Alfa Romeo also cut a good figure as a sedan (*below right*).

X-ray of the Alfa Romeo 156—the transversely mounted engine in front drives the front wheels. The rear axle is a multi-link construction for sporty handling.

total of over 670,000 examples were produced. The successor model was called the 159, and its unmistakable look was the work of new Alfa Romeo chief designer Wolfgang Egger. "A car must have a face," said the German director of *Centro Stile*. One look at the Alfa Romeo 159 is enough to understand what Egger meant by that.

Egger's team developed the design in cooperation with Giorgetto Giugiaro's Italdesign studio. The front area is dominated by the three round headlights, each joined together as a group of lights. The starting point for the interior design is the cockpit, which is tailored to the driver. Here, as in the Alfa Romeo Spider of the 1960s, the two large and centrally arranged round instruments for the speedometer and rev counter dominate.

As with its predecessor the Model 156, more than half of the Alfa Romeo 159 found its way into the Sportwagon estate version, which was also a joint production of Italdesign and the *Centro Stile Alfa Romeo*. The verdict of the public confirms that this cooperation has also paid off. The readers of the trade magazine *AutoBild* voted the Alfa Romeo 159 Sportwagon the "Most Beautiful Car in the World" in its category.

TWIN BROTHERS

From 1994, the Alfa Romeo Spider did almost everything differently than the original model from 1966. The design of the subsequent model series was even more radical—and the differences between it and the coupe dwindled.

From 2006, like the Brera Coupé, the Alfa Romeo Spider (previous spread) was based on the Model 159. The GTV (*right*) and Spider (*facing page*) versions of the preceding 916 series were technically independent.

At the end of the 1980s and the beginning of the 1990s, the market for convertibles changed dramatically. The days of the summer niche product for open-air fanatics were over. Buyers now also demanded all-season qualities from a roadster, and development costs for individual models were rising. More and more brands were offering convertibles that were technically heavily based on sedans.

Alfa Romeo bucked this trend and presented the next generation of the Spider in 1994, together with the coupe called the GTV (model series 916), which was almost identical except for the different roof shape. The design of both models was the result of a collaboration between the in-house *Centro Stile* and Studio Pininfarina. The pronounced wedge shape broke radically with the style of the preceding models, but it was definitely one thing: independent. Only the flat scudetto and the two narrow side air intakes invoked design icons from Alfa Romeo.

Completely new was the steeply rising sideline, which gave the twin brothers an emphatically dynamic look. Just like the two individual headlights on each side, it took up ideas from the *Proteo* concept study from 1991, which was created under the direction of then-Alfa Romeo design director Walter de Silva. To implement this shape perfectly, the engineers resorted to an elaborate design of the engine hood. Together with the upper third of the front fenders, it consisted of a single part that could be folded forward and was made of plastic, using a special process. The beading running across the flank to the rear end of the cockpit formed a collar that protectively surrounded the passengers. The soft top disappeared completely under a cover, a first for an Alfa Romeo Spider. A band of lights running across the entire rear of the vehicle ensured family resemblance.

The Alfa Romeo Spider and Alfa Romeo GTV also demonstrated a great deal of independence under their unusually wide bodies. It's true that the front-wheel drive system, including transversely mounted engines, displayed similarities to the 164 and 155 sedan models. The chassis, however, was a completely separate development and ensured convincingly sporty handling.

In 2003, the Spider and GTV received a redesigned front end with a larger, chrome radiator grille. The production figures show that both models met the expectations placed in them; by 2004, more than 80,000 units had rolled off the production line at the Alfa Romeo plant at Arese and at Pininfarina.

AR SPIDER

In keeping with tradition, Alfa Romeo worked with Giugiaro on the design of the Brera. The studio had often designed coupes for the brand in the past.

The next generation of the Alfa Romeo Spider (model series 939), unveiled in 2006, was also designed in collaboration between *Centro Stile Alfa Romeo* and Pininfarina. The Italian body maker was also responsible for production. Technically, the new Alfa Romeo Spider, just like the *Brera* coupe named after a Turin suburb, was largely based on the 159 Sedan.

A striking styling element of the Spider and *Brera* was the three round headlights on each side, whose diameter increased slightly from the inside to the outside. Visually, they converged on the vertical radiator grille with the fully chromed *scudetto*. The two trapezoidal halves of the radiator grille were divided horizontally by a fine trim strip reminiscent of the chrome bumper on the 1966 Alfa Romeo Spider.

The taillights invoked the look of the front headlights. Below the license plate, which was integrated into the rear apron, the darkly contrasted diffuser is framed by four chrome-plated exhaust tailpipes–the Alfa Romeo Spider and Alfa Romeo *Brera* were automobiles with sporty aspirations.

The special dynamics of both models were also reflected in the elongated hood, the distinctive shoulder line, and the pronounced rear fenders.

Like its historical predecessors, this Alfa Romeo Spider relied on a classic soft top that could be fully retracted electro-hydraulically.

The roofline of the Spider with the top closed was almost identical to that of the steel-roofed *Brera*. When the Spider's soft top was folded back–electro-hydraulically–two rollover bars marked the silhouette of the "Convertible of the Year 2006." Like small hoods, "cups" behind them assumed the shape of the headrests and let them flow harmoniously into the roof cover.

Powerful engines gave the Roadster and the Coupé a superior performance. The range included two technical innovations. For the first time in its history, the Alfa Romeo Spider wa also available with a turbodiesel powerplant that produced 200 hp for a top speed of 141.7 mph (228 kph). The six-cylinder 3.2 JTS V6 24V was combined with four-wheel drive.

This was worthwhile, as are electronic driving assistance systems. With 260 hp, the most powerful version of the last Alfa Romeo Spider, built until 2010, was around two and a half times as powerful than the "*Duetto*" from 1966.

Like the original Spider, the 939 series Alfa Romeo Spider was designed by Pininfarina. The leather interior is spectacular.

The special "*Rosso Competizione*" (Competition Red) paint features a unique play of light and shadow (*above*). The eight-cylinder engine generates 450 hp from 4.7 liters of displacement (*below*).

BEAUTY AND THE BEAST

With an available 450 hp, the Alfa Romeo 8C *Competizione* plays in the league of super sports cars. At least equally breathtaking is the technically identical Spider.

The Alfa Romeo *8C Competizione* invokes design elements from the legendary *Tipo 33 Stradale* of 1967. Both have an eight-cylinder engine, but that of the *8C Competizione* produces almost twice as much power.

Competizione! Any questions? The fascination of the Alfa Romeo 8C *Competizione* begins with its name. "*Competizione*"–Italian for competition–was officially used as a designation for the racing version of a production model for the first time with the Alfa Romeo 6C 2500, driven by the later Formula 1 world champion Juan Manuel Fangio at the 1950 *Mille Miglia*. And 8C–an abbreviation for*otto cilindri* (eight cylinders)–refers to the legendary eight-cylinder engines from the 1930s. Designed by Vittorio Jano with a contemporary in-line design, they catapulted racing cars from Arese to victories in the twenty-four-hour race at Le Mans and at the *Mille Miglia* and *Targa Florio* road races several times.

And so the Alfa Romeo 8C *Competizione*, which enraptured the public at the 2006 Paris Motor Show, was designed to revive the Alfa Romeo spirit. The design was like a quiz on quotes from the brand's history. Wolfgang Egger, the German who was design director at Alfa Romeo in this era, clearly had a heart for automotive classics. And so did his boss, brand director Antonio Baravalle. He unceremoniously took the funds necessary for the development of the car from the advertising budget. "The Alfa Romeo 8C *Competizione* is the perfect advertisement," said Baravalle.

Egger further developed the show car shown three years earlier at the IAA in Frankfurt to series production readiness without touching its outstanding features. The headlights, which protrude slightly over the hood, resembled those of the *Tipo 33 Stradale* from 1967. The nearly vertical rear end–called a *coda tronca* in Italian–was reminiscent of the second series of the Alfa Romeo *Giulietta SZ* from 1961. The circular taillights are a homage to the *Giulia TZ*, which was one year younger and, like the *Giulietta SZ*, was a racing car. In short, the body of the Alfa Romeo 8C *Competizione*, made of carbon fiber-reinforced plastic, flirted with history, as if *Centro Stile* were paying tribute to an entire era of automotive design.

The dynamic lines were underlined by specially developed paints, including the presentation color "*Rosso Competizione*" (Competition Red). Seven coats of clear lacquer with admixed pigments in red and silver created a deep, shimmering red that highlighted the curves and contours and changes from silver to deep red depending on the incidence of light. More than half of the buyers opted for this color. The classic lines also continued in the interior, from the round digital instruments to milled aluminum trim, switches, and handles to leather-trimmed bucket seats.

Critics and fans were equally enthusiastic. Jeremy Clarkson, host of the British cult series *Top Gear*, called the Alfa Romeo 8C *Competizione* the "most beautiful automobile ever built." Even the show car shown in advance won the Design Award for Concept Cars & Prototypes at the famous Concours d'Elegance in Villa d'Este on Lake Como in 2004.

Like the coupé, the Alfa Romeo 8C Spider, which is largely identical mechanically, was built just 500 times. The sports seats are a highlight. The leather upholstery has a woven effect on the seat surface.

The special "*Rosso Competizione*" (Competition Red) paint features a unique play of light and shadow (*above*). The eight-cylinder engine generates 450 hp from 4.7 liters of displacement (*below*).

With its close-cut fabric top, the Alfa Romeo 8C Spider has a more elegant look than the very masculine coupe. Extravagant color combinations also contribute to this.

But the Alfa Romeo 8C *Competizione* also took up technical themes that were close to the brand's heart. The power source was an eight-cylinder naturally aspirated gasoline engine in a modern V construction. It produced 450 hp from a displacement of 4.7 liters.

This enabled acceleration from zero to 62 mph (100 kph) in 4.2 seconds and a top speed of just under 186 mph (300 kph), underpinned by the brand's own engine. The whole thing was accompanied by the sound of the highest super sports car perfection—the finest Italian *bel canto* (beautiful singing) came out of the four tailpipes.

The traditional transaxle configuration typical of the brand—engine at the front, six-speed gearbox shifted by paddles on the steering wheel at the rear axle—ensured optimum weight distribution. For the first time since the early 1990s, an Alfa Romeo production car was powered exclusively by the rear wheels. The number of units was limited to 500, with about eighty units going to Germany.

Quite a few of the interested parties also asked for a roadster version. With Alfa Romeo, they were preaching to the choir. The 8C Spider, whose production number was also limited to 500, was displayed at the 2008 Geneva Motor Show.

Although stylistically, the only difference from the coupe was the fabric roof, which fit snugly like a baseball cap, the 8C Spider had a much more feminine appearance. One reason was the different color palette—the open-air super sports car was particularly popular in the noble metallic paint colors *Bianco Madreperla* (white mother of pearl) and *Grigio Magnesio* (magnesium gray), combined with a red leather interior.

But the Alfa Romeo 8C *Competizione* and Alfa Romeo 8C Spider were far more than high-tech showpieces and finger exercises for the designers. The innovative design also gave a preview of the style elements and proportions of future models from the brand.

BROTHER LIGHTFOOT

Not just the design of the Alfa Romeo 4C is breathtaking. High-tech materials such as carbon fiber and aluminum lower the car's empty weight to a racing car-like 1,973 pounds (895 kg).

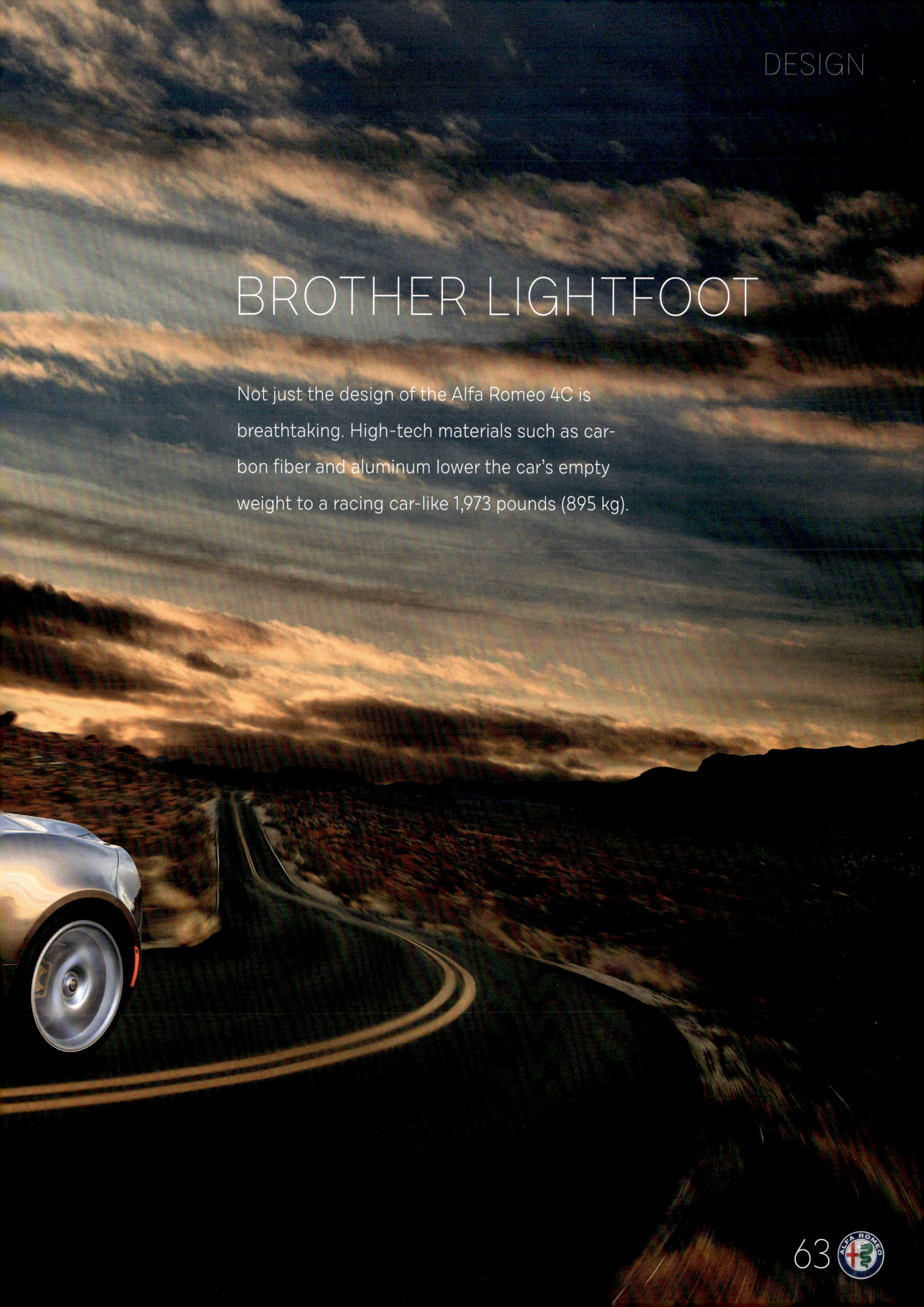

The engine, located behind the cockpit, ensures optimal weight distribution. The four-cylinder turbo produces 240 hp from a displacement of just 1.8 liters.

The search for the ultimate sports car has two basic solutions: high engine power or low weight. To a certain extent, both are mutually exclusive in a series-produced vehicle, because powerful engines are relatively large and therefore heavy, and the drive systems, chassis and braking systems they require must be correspondingly large and heavy.

The engineers took the first step in 2006 with the Alfa Romeo 8C *Competizione*. Its naturally aspirated V8 engine with a superior 450 hp was a statement. Despite extensive lightweight construction, the coupe weighed just under 3,527 pounds (1,600 kg)—a good figure in this class, but not exactly a lightweight.

Enter the Alfa Romeo 4C. As the abbreviation "4C" reveals, the engine had only half as many cylinders (*4 cilindri*) as that of the 8C *Competizione*. The output of the 1.8-liter turbo gasoline engine was also about half, at 240 hp. In order to achieve an impressive performance similar to that of the 8C *Competizione*, the designers chose the second approach—they made the car extremely lightweight.

To achieve this, they used ultralight high-tech materials derived from racing and space research. In the case of the Alfa Romeo 4C, for example, a so-called monocoque made of carbon fiber served as the load-bearing structure, similar to that of a Formula 1 racing car. Aluminum was used for the roll bar behind the cockpit, the front and rear subframes, and the chassis and brakes. The body was made of fiber-reinforced plastic composite material, which offered a weight advantage of around 20 percent over steel. There was even potential for savings in the glass for the windows. All the windows were 10 percent thinner on average, which corresponded to a weight reduction of about 15 percent.

The overall result was impressive. The Alfa Romeo 4C unveiled in 2013 weighed just 1,973 pounds (895 kg) ready to drive. Most city cars are heavier. In addition, the 4C achieved a power-to-weight ratio that was almost identical to that of its big brother, the Alfa Romeo 8C *Competizione*: in both models, which are completely different technologically, each horsepower had to move less than 8.8 pounds (4 kg) of vehicle weight.

The performance of the Alfa Romeo 4C was correspondingly sporty. Equipped with rear-wheel drive and a dual-clutch gearbox, the coupe accelerated from zero to 62 mph in 4.5 seconds. During emergency braking, deceleration forces of more than 1.2 g acted on the passengers, while lateral acceleration in curves reached up to 1.1 g.

Together with its mid-engine configuration—the turbo petrol engine is placed behind the cockpit—the lightweight materials of the Alfa Romeo 4C stood for a reduction to the essentials, a concept also followed by the designers of the *Centro Stile*. The result was an extremely compact

The proportions are right; the dimensions are extremely compact. The Alfa Romeo 4C's plastic body is just under 13 feet (4 meters) long and 46.5 inches (118 cm) high.

The Alfa Romeo 4C Spider is technically identical to the coupe. The removable roof is made of carbon fiber. Special models (*right*, the Spider Italia) are highly sought after.

sports car with a length of just under 13 feet (4 meters), a width of 78.7 inches (200 cm), a height of 46.5 inches (118 cm), and a wheelbase of 94.5 inches (240 cm).

The body enclosed the vehicle's technology like a well-fitting glove. The sculptural hood was characterized by the V-shaped dome, which ended in the triangular radiator opening at the front. The main headlights were recessed into the fenders. The side of the car was divided by a bead that ran into the air intakes in the rear fenders. These openings supplied fresh air to the intake system and the intercooler.

The rear of the vehicle was particularly important. The pronounced mudguards directed the view toward the rear window, under which the engine was freely visible. The round taillights were protected by the rear apron. The lower end of the apron was formed by a diffuser, which ensured clean airflow at the rear axle and track stability at high speeds. In fact, the aerodynamics of the Alfa Romeo 4C generated downforce above a certain speed—just as you would expect from a racing car.

The no-frills design language and high-tech materials also characterized the cockpit. Like a racing car, the carbon-fiber monocoque was freely visible in some places. Trim was fitted only where it is absolutely necessary. Details made of aluminum and bucket seats underlined the racing effect.

From 2015, the Alfa Romeo 4C would also be available as a Spider with a removable roof. Both body variants inspired various special models. The Alfa Romeo 4C *Competizione* was available exclusively in the body color *Grigio Vesuvio Opaco* (Matte Vesuvius Gray). The Alfa Romeo 4C Spider Italia appeared particularly elegant and exclusive with the body color *Blu Misano Metallic* (Metallic Misano Blue), among others.

The Alfa Romeo 4C was good for the brand's image in Europe. Perhaps even more important, with both variants, Alfa Romeo returned to the USA in 2015, after a twenty-year break. Although the Alfa Romeo 8C *Competizione* would also be sold in the United States in the meantime, it was sold through the Maserati network. A separate dealership structure was being created for the Alfa Romeo 4C.

Thanks to its carbon-fiber monocoque, the Alfa Romeo 4C Spider requires hardly any additional stiffening in the body. The headlights are a work of art in themselves.

DOUBLE COMEBACK

The Alfa Romeo *Giulia* not only marks the return of a great name, but also the revival of the tradition-rich letter combination GTA.

In the 1960s, the *Giulia* model shaped Alfa Romeo's reputation in a direction that still determines how the brand is seen around the world today. Expectations were correspondingly high when a new *Giulia* (model series 952) was launched in 2016. The sedan with the classic notchback layout perfectly embodied the concept of *la Meccanica delle Emozioni*, or "the Mechanics of Emotions." And it was a success: the *Giulia* was showered with international awards.

The body, designed at *Centro Stile Alfa Romeo*, showed proportions that were an expression of the technical layout. The *Giulia*, which is based on the specially developed *Giorgio* platform, relied on classic rear-wheel drive—at least in most model variants. Another core element, which was also expressed visually, was the vehicle's almost 50:50 weight distribution. In order to balance the vehicle weight optimally, the engine and the most important mechanical components were placed between the axles. The result was short body overhangs at the front and rear, a rearward passenger compartment, and pronounced rear fenders.

This layout resulted in the longest wheelbase in the segment, combined with comparatively compact dimensions. The streamlined profile was strongly reminiscent of the design of one of the most beautiful cars of all time—the Alfa Romeo *Giulietta Sprint* of the 1950s.

In positioning the *Giulia*, Alfa Romeo cleverly relied on the charisma of the top model, the *Quadrifoglio*. Under its hood is a 510hp (375 kW) V-6 bi-turbo gasoline engine, to which Ferrari contributed Formula 1 know-how. The 2.9-liter (177 cu. in.) engine enabled a top speed of 190.7 mph (307 kph) and acceleration from zero to 62 mph in 3.9 seconds. Even before its official market launch, the Alfa Romeo *Giulia Quadrifoglio* completed a record-breaking drive that caused quite a stir in the scene. The sedan with the legendary four-leaf clover on its flanks rounded the famous Nordschleife of the Nürburgring with a new class record time.

Even the less powerful model variants shone with motorsport-inspired technology. The driveshaft, hood, and roof all were made of carbon fiber. In addition to the engine, the brakes, the wheel suspensions (including the front strut domes), and the front and rear subframes were made of aluminum. Some body parts such as doors and fenders were also made of this lightweight metal. Further weight was saved by optional brake discs made of ceramic-carbon fiber composite material and seat frames made of carbon fiber.

In 2020, Alfa Romeo went one better—the V-6 bi-turbo petrol engine in the *Giulia GTA* and *Giulia GTAm* models produced an impressive 540 hp (397 kW). But more

The limited-edition Alfa Romeo *Giulia GTAm* (*previous spread*) offers bucket seats, while leather is the order of the day on the standard model. The color *Giallo Ocra* (ocher yellow, *below left*) invokes the "Bertone" from the 1960s.

The top production model–the Alfa Romeo *Giulia Quadrifoglio*, has 510 hp under the hood (*above*). The same engine is also available in the special NRING model (*below*), a homage to the Nürburgring.

The Alfa Romeo *Giulia* is designed as a classic sedan with rear-wheel drive. However, some model versions also offer all-wheel drive. All have a carbon-fiber driveshaft, hood, and roof.

horsepower isn't everything; at the same time, vehicle weight was reduced by around 220 pounds (100 kg). The legendary abbreviation GTA was therefore fully justified.

The three letters stand for the Italian term *Gran Turismo Alleggerita* (Lightweight Grand Touring) and describe a fast touring car (*Gran Turismo*) with lightweight construction (*Alleggerita*). Alfa Romeo first used this abbreviation in 1965 for the *Giulia Sprint GTA*. The vehicle, which was designed as a basic model for motorsport, had, among other things, a body made of aluminum. The further developed version with thick fender extensions was given the suffix GTAm. Alfa Romeo won three European Touring Car Championship titles and dozens of national championships with the various racing versions of the *Giulia GTA* in the late 1960s and early 1970s.

And like its historic predecessor, the 2020 Alfa Romeo *Giulia GTA* was put through a weight reduction process and its aerodynamics optimized. The engineers also benefited from the knowledge they gained in Formula 1 together with their partner Sauber. While the optimization of the *Giulia GTA* concentrated on increasing the engine's performance, the *Giulia GTAm* went a few steps further. The active front splitter was larger than on the *Quadrifoglio* and GTA. To maintain the aerodynamic balance of the entire car, especially at high speeds, a large carbon-fiber rear spoiler increased downforce at the rear axle. The same idea was behind the design of the active front splitter, side skirts, rear spoiler, and carbon-fiber diffuser. The 1.97-inch (50 mm) wider track on the front and rear axles and the bulbous flared fenders are strongly reminiscent of the historic *Giulia GTAm*.

In the interior, bucket seats, six-point seat belts, roll bars, and carbon-fiber trim created a racing atmosphere. Instead of a rear seat, there were holders for two helmets and fire extinguishers. The rear windows were made of lightweight Lexan. The doors were closed with straps, which also saved a few ounces.

While the newly reissued, historic colors *Giallo Ocra* (Yellow Ochre) and *Verde Visconti* (Visconti Green) were available for all models of the Alfa Romeo *Giulia*, a special highlight was the paint finish in the style of the racing cars from the 1960s, which was available only on the GTA and GTAm. Back then, different colored masks in front enabled the mechanics in the pits to identify the cars of the various drivers. In other respects, too, both special models were hard to beat in terms of exclusivity. Altogether, just 500 examples of the Alfa Romeo *Giulia GTA* and *GTAm* were built.

THE S IN SUV

Not everything that nowadays is called a "Sports Utility Vehicle" is in fact sporty. The Alfa Romeo *Stelvio*, however, justifiably bears this name.

STELVIO
U DUBAI 66508

The Alfa Romeo *Stelvio* is named after the *Passo dello Stelvio* (Stelvio Pass) in the Alps. The body of the brand's first SUV was designed by American Scott Krugger (*below*).

The *Nordschleife* of the Nürburgring, one of the oldest, most famous, and most demanding racetracks in the world, is also considered the ultimate challenge for every sporty production car. All of the major car makers regularly test their products on the hill-and-dale track in the Eifel region, which was opened in 1927 and is still over 12.4 miles (20 km) long today. A lap record–in the respective segment–is an accolade for new vehicle models and is recognized accordingly by the scene. Alfa Romeo has achieved this feat with the *Giulia* sedan. In September 2017, a test driver again set out on the hunt for better times. This time, he raced an Alfa Romeo *Stelvio* through the "green hell," as former Formula 1 world champion Jacky Stewart once called the *Nordschleife*. In the end, the stopwatches stopped at exactly 7:51.7 minutes–a new lap record for SUVs.

With this feat, the engineers at Alfa Romeo had proven that they take the term SUV seriously. After all, it stands for "Sports Utility Vehicle" (i.e., a multi-purpose vehicle with sporty characteristics). By this definition, the *Stelvio*, sold from 2017, was the first SUV in Alfa Romeo's history. There was no comparison to the AR51 off-road vehicle of the 1950s. The "*Matta*," the crazy one, was indeed anything but sporty.

The model name *Stelvio* is a tribute to the highest paved pass in the Italian Alps–the *Stilfser Joch*, or *Stelvio* in Italian. The "*Strada Statale 38 dello Stelvio*" (State Road 38 *Stelvio*) offers around seventy-five hairpin curves, breathtaking views, and in places, a gradient of more than 7 percent up to the top of the pass at 9,048 feet ASL (2,758 meters) on its most beautiful 12.4 miles (20 km). After it was opened in 1826, it became one of the most important traffic and freight routes between Austria and Italy for more than a century. The Stelvio road is used today as a merciless test track for automobiles, just like the *Nordschleife* at the Nürburgring.

Choosing this legendary pass as the model name showed a good deal of self-confidence. In fact, the Alfa Romeo *Stelvio* was built on the same technical platform as the *Giulia*, including a carbon-fiber driveshaft and aluminum doors and hood. It thus provided the basis for sporty driving performance.

Alfa Romeo chief designer Scott Krugger also gave the *Stelvio* an emphatically dynamic look that embodies strength, dynamism, and compactness even when stationary. The body showed fundamental building blocks of Italian design: an unerring sense of proportion and stylistic straightforwardness. The headlights were low and narrowly drawn together, giving the *Stelvio*'s face an almost aggressive look. The shape of the front and rear fenders emphasized the car's muscular appearance.

Spectacular special models–the Alfa Romeo *Stelvio Quadrifoglio NRING* pays homage to the Nürburgring (*top left*), while the Alfa Romeo Racing version was developed together with the Alfa Romeo Formula 1 team.

With electronically controlled four-wheel drive, the Alfa Romeo *Stelvio* also cuts a fine figure off the beaten track. However, the 4x4 traction primarily ensures sporty handling on the road.

Nevertheless, Krugger also paid attention to feminine accents in the lines. Indentations on the flank gave the Alfa Romeo Stelvio a sexy waistline. The elaborate three-dimensionality of the flanks also created exciting light-shadow effects. In terms of the sideline, the SUV looked more like a mid-size sedan due to its flat roofline and sloping rear. The pronounced shoulders above the wheel wells were reminiscent of the shape of Alfa Romeo sports cars of the 1960s.

Like the *Giulia*, the *Stelvio* also received the high-performance *Quadrifoglio* variant as its flagship. Its heart was also the V-6 bi-turbo engine, made almost entirely of aluminum, which produced 510 hp (375 kW) from 2.9 liters of displacement. With this engine under the hood, coupled with an eight-speed automatic transmission, the Alfa Romeo *Stelvio Quadrifoglio* reached a top speed of 175.8 mph (283 kph) and accelerated from zero to 62 mph (100 kph) in 3.8 seconds. It was exactly the right equipment for the previously mentioned SUV lap record on the *Nordschleife*.

The Alfa Romeo *Stelvio* received numerous design awards. The *Stelvio*'s image as an Italian style icon in the SUV sector was fueled by special models, in which design plays a major role in the equipment. In this respect, the *Stelvio* and *Giulia* each ran in pairs. A tribute to the Nürburgring was the Alfa Romeo *Stelvio Quadrifoglio NRING*, of which just 108 were produced in 2018 to mark the brand's 108th birthday. Its exclusive matte gray "*Grigio Circuito*" (Circuit Gray) paintwork, carbon-fiber exterior mirror caps, V-shaped carbon-fiber insert in the radiator grille, and side skirts with carbon-fiber inserts looked sporty and elegant at the same time.

With only ten examples each of the *Stelvio* and *Giulia* models, the "Alfa Romeo Racing" edition (2019) was even more strictly limited. This special model paid homage to Alfa Romeo's involvement in Formula 1, the number produced representing the brand's ten victories in Grand Prix racing in the 1950s.

Based on the *Quadrifoglio* variant, the Alfa Romeo *Stelvio "Alfa Romeo Racing"* was available exclusively in the *bicolore* (two-tone) paint finish. The combination of "Trofeo White" and "Competition Red" was reminiscent of the 2019 cars of the Formula 1 team Alfa Romeo Racing. Just in case anyone should still have any doubts about the consistent sportiness of the *Stelvio* . . .

The Alfa Romeo *Stelvio Quadrifoglio* is the only production model powered by a V-6 turbo with 510 hp (*below*). All model versions come with noble materials in the interior (*above left*).

MEN BEHIND THE MYTH

Over the past 110 years, a whole series of engineers, businessmen, and managers have shaped the destiny of Alfa Romeo. The foundation stone was laid in Milan on June 24, 1910.

1

2

***Photos above and on the following page*: Nicola Romeo (1), Giuseppe Merosi (2), Vittorio Jano (3), Ugo Gobbato (4) and Orazio Satta Puliga (5, with the Alfa Romeo *Tipo 158* Grand Prix car)**

Today, one would possibly speak of a hostile takeover: a group of businessmen buys a factory in Portello, a district of Milan, from the Italian branch of the French automobile brand Darracq, which is facing bankruptcy. On June 24, 1910, the management officially renamed the company *Società Anonima Lombarda Fabbrica Automobili* with the four letters A.L.F.A. as its abbreviation. The *Società Anonima Lombarda Fabbrica Automobili* was renamed Alfa Romeo–today one of the best-known automobile brands in the world–after the Neapolitan entrepreneur **Nicola Romeo** (1876-1938) joined the company.

A.L.F.A.'s first chief designer was **Giuseppe Merosi** (1872-1956). The surveyor from Piacenza gained experience at Bianchi and Fiat. His first work in Portello was the *Tipo 24 HP*. This model was not only exceptionally elegant, its 4.1-liter four-cylinder engine producing 42 hp also made possible a top speed of 62.4 mph (100 kph)–an impressive figure for the time.

Merosi also recognized that success in motorsport was good advertising for the company's products. He not only designed racing versions of the A.L.F.A. series models, but also a full-fledged Grand Prix vehicle. Its engine featured dual ignition and dual overhead camshafts, two technologies that would play a major role in the history of the brand.

With its range of exclusive luxury automobiles, A.L.F.A. ran into economic difficulties during the First World War. Nicola Romeo, a businessman from Naples in southern Italy, seized this opportunity. Romeo, a mechanical engineer by training, had grown wealthy producing equipment for the mining industry. He switched production in Portello to the manufacture of engines, superchargers, and other components for military purposes.

Romeo took over the majority of shares in the now prospering company and returned to building cars after the end of the war. These now bore the brand name "Alfa Romeo." The *Tipo 20-30 HP*, designed by Giuseppe Merosi in 1920, was the first model with this logo on its radiator grille. Romeo left the management of the company in 1928.

Alfa Romeo also returned to racing after the Great War. The great successes came with **Vittorio Jano** (1891-1965). The engineer with Hungarian roots and a past at Fiat designed, among other things, the eight-cylinder in-line engine of the *Tipo P2*, with which Alfa Romeo won the first-ever automobile world championship in 1925. But Jano's production engines also set the trend for Alfa Romeo's model range in the decades to come. The six-cylinder *Tipo 6C 1500*, with which Alfa Romeo achieved its first victory in the prestigious *Mille Miglia* road race in 1928, was characterized by a cylinder head made of light metal, overhead valves, two overhead camshafts, and centrally positioned spark plugs.

However, Alfa Romeo was unable to convert its victories on the world's racetracks into profitable sales of production cars. In 1933, the company had to be saved from bankruptcy

by the state-owned *Istituto per la Ricostruzione Industriale* (Institute for Industrial reconstruction, or IRI). The IRI appointed **Ugo Gobbato** (1888-1945) to reorganize the company. With relevant experience at Fiat, where he managed the construction of production plants in Lingotto/Turin and Moscow, Gobbato built the first Alfa Romeo plant outside Milan. From 1938 onwards, however, the factory at Pomigliano d'Arco near Naples did not produce cars, but instead aero-engines. The approaching Second World War was undoubtedly casting its shadow.

A bombing raid in 1943 largely destroyed the main factory in Portello. It was not until 1946 that the company, now called Alfa Romeo S.p.A., resumed operations. The technical director during this era was **Orazia Satta Puliga** (1910-1974). The mechanical and aeronautical engineer had already been working in the development department since 1938 and was promoted to chief designer in 1946. In 1951, he was promoted to General Manager and became Vice President in 1969.

Under Satta Puliga's direction, Alfa Romeo won two world championships in the newly founded Formula 1. He was also responsible for the 1900, *Giulietta*, *Giulia*, *Montreal*, and *Alfetta* production models. The *Giulia* was built at the Arese plant on the outskirts of Milan, which opened in 1961. It achieved the breakthrough long sought after by Alfa Romeo, including on the export market.

An important factor in the *Giulia*'s success was its four-cylinder engine, which, with its light-alloy cylinder head

***From left*: Orazio Satta Puliga, engine designer Giuseppe Busso, Giuseppe Luraghi, and Carlo Chiti, the head of Autodelta, at a reception in 1971**

***Above and top of following page*: director Giuseppe Luraghi (1) with Alfa Romeo factory driver Teodore Zeccoli (1969), Vittorio Ghidella (2), and Rudolf Hruska (3), the man behind the *Alfasud* project**

and twin overhead camshafts, could not deny its racing heritage. This engine was the masterpiece of **Giuseppe Busso** (1913-2006).

Born in Turin, he had already been at Alfa Romeo once, from 1939 to 1946, but at that time as an engine designer in the racing department. After two years at Ferrari, Busso returned to Alfa Romeo in 1948, now in series development. Among the milestones of his time as chief engineer, apart from the four-cylinder engine first used in the 1900 and *Giulietta* models, known to fans as the "twin-cam," was a six-cylinder engine that is still revered today as the "*Busso V6*." The silky-smooth engine was used in the *Sei*, GTV6, and 75 models, among others, and survived in further developed form into the 2000s.

Satta Puliga, as director and vice-president of Alfa Romeo, was not alone in transforming the company from an exclusive small-series manufacturer into a large-scale car maker. **Giuseppe Luraghi** (1905-1991) was an important partner. From 1951, he was general director of Finmeccanica, the arm of the IRI responsible for holdings in the mechanical engineering sector. From 1960 onwards, Luraghi, who also made a name for himself as a writer, was also managing director of Alfa Romeo. This period saw the construction of the new Arese plant and the expansion of the aero-engine factory at Pomigliano d'Arco to include a car plant. A completely new model was to be produced there—the *Alfasud*. Luraghi entrusted the entire project to the Austrian engineer **Rudolf Hruska** (1915-1995).

Hruska had already been at Alfa Romeo from 1954 to 1959, after working in the development office of Ferdinand Porsche, Abarth, Cisitalia's Formula 1 project, and Finmeccanica. Together with Satta Puliga, he developed the *Giulietta* model. Interrupted by a period at Simca and Fiat, Hruska returned to Alfa Romeo in 1967 and was given responsibility for the *Alfasud*. He developed the first Alfa Romeo with front-wheel drive to enter series production. Gioretto Giugiaro was responsible for the design of the car.

When the state-owned IRI decided to sell Alfa Romeo at the beginning of the 1980s, **Vittorio Ghidella** (1931-2011) took action. Ghidella had previously built Fiat into Europe's second-largest manufacturer, in whose portfolio the sporty Alfa Romeo brand fit perfectly. After 52 years, Alfa Romeo was once again privately owned as part of the new *Alfa Lancia Industriale S.p.A.*

As a statement of the company's reawakened efficiency, Ghidella approved the Alfa Romeo SZ (1989) sports car, limited to 1,000 units. Its unmistakable appearance, co-developed by Zagato, made the coupé and the Alfa Romeo RZ roadster (1992), which was presented shortly afterward, into flagships of the brand. However, the new large Alfa Romeo 164 sedan (1987) was more important from an economic point of view. It was the product of a development partnership with Fiat, Lancia, and Saab. The mid-size 155 sedan (1992), the sporty 145 small family car (1994), and its five-door counterpart the 146 (1995) were also based on a platform developed jointly with Fiat.

Just how independent Alfa Romeo remained under the direction of Fiat was demonstrated by the 156 model, which thrilled fans and the trade public at the 1997 Frankfurt Motor Show. The Alfa Romeo 156 also broke new ground in the technology sector. For the first time in the world, a series-produced vehicle was equipped with common-rail direct injection technology, an Alfa Romeo invention that would revolutionize the diesel engine in the years to come.

In 2003, a man took the helm of Fiat S.p.A. and Fiat Group Automobiles who would determine the company's fortunes for 15 years–**Sergio Marchionne** (1952-2018). The Italian-Canadian focused on expansion. In 2005, he merged Alfa Romeo with Maserati to form a luxury division. In 2007, Alfa Romeo Automobiles S.p.A. became independent again, wholly owned by Fiat Group Automobiles.

Through the merger with the U.S. company Chrysler, Marchionne formed Fiat Chrysler Automobiles (FCA) in 2014. In addition to Alfa Romeo, FCA also included the Italian brands Fiat, Abarth, Fiat Professional (vans), and Lancia as well as the American brands Chrysler, Jeep, Dodge, and RAM. As part of this group of companies, Alfa Romeo has firmly established itself as the sportiest Italian mass-produced brand. (With the merger between FCA and the French PSA Group in 2021, the multinational automotive corporation Stellantis N.V. was formed.)

The founding of Fiat Chrysler Automobiles (FCA) took place during the era of Sergio Marchionne (pictured in 2017 at the press conference announcing Alfa Romeo's reentry into Formula 1).

ON LAND, ON WATER, AND IN THE AIR

It's no joke: for decades Alfa Romeo also produced trucks and buses. The company's high-performance racing engines have also won records in boating. And for a time, the company made the most money by producing aero engines.

***Previous spread*: At Pomigliano d'Arco in the south of Italy, Alfa Romeo built aero engines, initially for propeller-driven aircraft, but later jet engines as well.**

The first person to come up with the idea of installing an Alfa Romeo–or A.L.F.A.–engine in an aircraft was racing driver Nino Franchini. In November 1910, the Italian made a short hop in a biplane powered by the four-cylinder *Tipo 24 HP* outside Milan.

However, the company did not produce significant numbers of aircraft engines until the First World War. Like many car manufacturers, production at A.L.F.A. was switched to military machines. Even after the end of the war, aircraft engines were built at Portello, under license from British aero engine producers Bristol and Armstrong-Siddeley, among others. It was not until 1932 that the company, now renamed Alfa Romeo, presented its first in-house development, the nine-cylinder D2 radial engine designed by Vittorio Jano.

In the world economic crisis of the 1930s, sales at Alfa Romeo, which made only exclusive luxury cars at the time, collapsed dramatically. When the state-owned Institute for Industrial Reconstruction (IRI) took over the company in 1933, the new management focused increasingly on industrial sectors outside the automobile industry. The D2 radial engine was used by a number of aircraft manufacturers worldwide. During this time, the engine also made a name for itself through involvement in record-setting flights. The development of high-performance engines for aircraft also led to innovative processes and materials that were subsequently used in automobiles, including the light alloy Duralfa.

At one point, more than three-quarters of Alfa Romeo's revenue came from aircraft engines. This expansion–and the preparation for an apparently unavoidable second world war–made it possible for the company to build a factory at Pomigliano d'Arco in southern Italy. In 1941, the independent company Alfa Romeo Avio was founded there.

Air raids inflicted severe damage on the plants at Portello and Pomigliano d'Arco during the Second World War. In the postwar years, the plant in southern Italy was converted to produce trucks, buses, diesel engines, generators, and marine engines. The workers at Pomigliano d'Arco now repaired only aero engines.

It was not until the end of the 1940s that Alfa Romeo again expanded its involvement in the aircraft sector. In cooperation with Fiat, SAI Ambrosino, and Aermacchi, it produced aircraft such as the famous "*Angelo dei bimbi*" (Angel of the Children). In 1949, the small SAI Ambrosini 1001 *Grifo* (Griffon) aircraft, powered by an Alfa Romeo 110 engine, flew from Milan first to Buenos Aires in Argentina and then through South America to collect donations for the reconstruction of children's hospitals in Italy.

In the 1950s, Alfa Romeo also produced jet engines at Pomigliano d'Arco in collaboration with Fiat, albeit on a smaller scale. It was not until a decade later that this production became more important. Alfa Romeo became involved in the production of power plants for the Fiat G91 and the Lockheed F-104 Starfighter used by NATO countries, including the Federal Republic of Germany. In the 1970s, Alfa Romeo repaired and maintained Avio engines for Alitalia and the Italian air Force, among others. As the result of a cooperative agreement with Rolls-Royce, the number of employees at Pomigliano d'Arco increased to around 2,000. In 1979, Alfa Romeo became the first Italian company to produce turboprop engines. From 1982 on, Alfa Romeo Avio was gradually sold to Aeritalia, which in turn became part of Fiat Avio in 1996.

The fact that A.L.F.A. and later Alfa Romeo built powerful engines is proven by their success in motor racing. So the idea of installing these power plants in racing boats was obvious. The designers did not even stop at the eight-cylinder engines of the Formula 1 world champions, the

The Alfa Romeo Series 129 aero engine was a nine-cylinder radial, designed for a flight altitude of up to 3,200 meters.

The racing boat Arno II was powered by an eight-cylinder engine from the Tipo 158 Grand Prix racing car (*in the foreground*). Achille Gastoldi set a world speed record with it in 1940.

Tipo 158 and *Tipo 159 Alfetta*, and even the twelve-cylinder 12C Grand Prix engine. The four-, six- and eight-cylinder engines that powered the *Giulia GTA*, *6C 2500,* and *Tipo 33* models also found their way into racing boats.

From the 1920s to the 1980s, Alfa Romeo boat engines were involved in numerous speed records. In the 1940s, Achille Castoldi was a star of the big international boat races with his *Arno II*, which was powered by a 1.5-liter supercharged engine from the *Alfetta* and reached speeds of around 124.25 mph (200 kph). The *Arno II* was the first boat of its kind in the world. Castoldi's Scuderia Ambrosiana team, factory-supported by Alfa Romeo, even tested a twelve-cylinder aircraft engine from the brand with an impressive displacement of 2,075 cubic inches (34 liters).

A few years later, Milanese silk manufacturer and racing boat world champion Mario Verga was chasing records. His boat *Laura*, powered by two *Alfetta* engines, reached 180.2 mph (290 kph). However, Verga was killed in a record attempt on Lake Iseo in 1954. In 1969, Leopoldo Casanova set a new record in this boat class with the *Popoli-Alfa Romeo*, reaching 140 mph (225 kph). The boat, complete with its eight-cylinder *Tipo 33* racing engine prepared by Autodelta, can be seen today in the Alfa Romeo factory museum in Arese.

Less about speed was another less well-known Alfa Romeo division—heavy commercial vehicles. The F12 (1966) and AR6 (1982, based on the Fiat Ducato) vans, which are occasionally seen at classic car meets, were descendants of a whole fleet of trucks and buses whose origins go back to 1930.

In the global economic crisis of the time, sales at Alfa Romeo, which concentrated exclusively on exclusive luxury cars, collapsed dramatically. When the state-owned Institute for Industrial Reconstruction (IRI) took over Alfa Romeo, the new men at the top restructured the company in line with the government's push to build commercial vehicles. Alfa Romeo began producing chassis for trucks and buses. Since there was a lack of appropriate know-how, the company entered into cooperative ventures. The diesel engines were built under license from the German manufacturer Deutz, while Büssing-NAG supplied the chassis for the trucks.

Soon, design and technology became more independent. The Alfa Romeo engineers experimented with gasoline

From the 1920s to the 1980s, boat engines produced by Alfa Romeo were involved in numerous records and championships (in the photo is an event poster from 1941).

The Alfa Romeo 455 was a versatile truck with a payload of 5 tons (4.5 metric tons). The Alfa Romeo racing team liked to use it to transport Grand Prix and touring cars.

engines and developed special military models for use in Italy's African colonial territories. At the same time, the company also made elegant buses.

In the late 1930s, Alfa Romeo expanded its range to include light trucks, which were now powered by diesel engines developed in-house. After the Second World War, Alfa Romeo moved its commercial vehicle production from its main plant at Portello, Milan, to Pomigliano d'Arco near Naples. In 1958, the Mille model went into production. It offered modern technology such as power steering, an air-assisted clutch, and a synchronized ZF split gearbox for shifting even half gears. But in the long run, even this model did not stand a chance against the models made by larger competitors such as Fiat. In 1964, Alfa Romeo ceased truck production, at least at its own plant.

But the story was not over yet. The French manufacturer SAVIEM continued to use the Alfa Romeo name for light trucks in some countries until 1974. The Brazilian brand FNM has been manufacturing Alfa Romeo trucks under license since 1953. In 1968 Alfa Romeo took over the majority of shares in FNM, and the Mille model was relaunched for South America. It was not until FNM became part of Fiat together with Alfa Romeo in 1986 that the commercial vehicle era of Alfa Romeo was finally history.

The production of buses under the Alfa Romeo name ended some years ago. From the 1930s until the mid-1960s, the company also built chassis for various types of buses. Fitted with bodies from external manufacturers, they were a common sight on the streets of Italy, Uruguay, Sweden, Greece, and, during the Second World War, even some German cities. The range also includes such specialties as electrically powered trolley buses.

The Alfa Romeo 455 was a versatile truck with a payload of 5 tons (4.5 metric tons). The Alfa Romeo racing team liked to use it to transport Grand Prix and touring cars.

Sporty travel: From 1940 to 1964, Alfa Romeo also built omnibuses, around 5,000 in total. They were exported as far as South Africa and South America.

VISION FIRST

When it came to concept cars, Alfa Romeo and the design studios associated with the brand cast bold glances into the future. They have not always been as bold as hoped, however.

In 1971, Giugario surprised with the *Caimano* show car (*right and on the previous spread*). It was technically based on the *Alfasud*.

Show cars, studies, and concept cars with the Alfa Romeo logo on the radiator have a long tradition. Strictly speaking, the *Tipo HP40-60 Aerodinamica* of 1913 as well as the touring masterpieces the *6C 1750 Flying Star* (1931), the *6C 2500 Villa d'Este* (1949) and the *C52 Disco Volante* (1952) fall into this category.

Franco Scaglione, who worked for Bertone in the early 1950s, took the theme to a completely new level. With three futuristic *Berlinetta Aerodinamica Tecnica* (Berlinetta Technical Aerodynamics (BAT for short) concept cars, the Italian established his reputation as a star designer. Outstanding drag coefficients of 0.19 to 0.21 were measured for the BAT 5, BAT 7, and BAT 9. There were never plans for a production version, another typical feature of a concept car.

This was also true of the *Scarabeo* concept car, which Alfa Romeo unveiled at the 1966 Paris Motor Show. Like the Tipo 33, which was developed at the same time, it had an H-shaped tubular chassis. However, the engine was not the V-8 of the *Tipo 33*, but the aluminum four-cylinder from the *Giulia GTA*, installed transversely behind the cockpit.

The body, with its long, extremely flat snout; its cockpit set far back; and its short, crested rear, was designed by *Officine Stampaggi Industriali* (Industrial Molding Workshops, or OSI) at Borgaro Torinese. There were no doors; to get in, the roof and sides, which incorporated the windshield, were folded forward, not unlike the canopies of some aircraft.

OSI built two more variants of the *Scarabeo*. The second coupe was strongly reminiscent of the *Giulia TZ* but still had the engine behind the cockpit. A Spider version would have made a good racing car; however, the necessary design work was never completed.

The show effect of the glass cockpit was taken up by Giorgetto Giugiaro in 1971. His studio Ital Design, which was also responsible for the design of the *Alfasud*, surprised the public with the *Caimano* concept car at the Turrin Motor Show. It is hard to believe that underneath the wedge-shaped body was the shortened chassis of an *Alfasud*. The *Caimano* was intended to draw attention to the sporting qualities of the brand's first front-wheel-drive vehicle.

The instruments are just as futuristic as the Plexiglas cockpit. Instead of pointers, the scales behind them move. The strangely designed rims are intended to distract from the round tires—Giugiaro went right to the edge.

The second variant of the *Scarabeo* was similar to the Alfa Romeo *Giulia TZ* in some ways, but its chassis came from the *Tipo 33*. Like the first version (*below*), the OSI used the engine from the *Giulia GTA*.

BY POPULAR DEMAND

Sometimes concept cars make it into series production. The public just has to demand it loudly enough.

The prototype, here before it was named the Montreal (*also on the previous spread*), was flown to Montreal for Expo 67.

The call from Montreal came as a surprise to the Alfa Romeo management. The organizers of the 1967 World's Fair in the Canadian city wanted to highlight the theme of "Man and his World" in a wide variety of areas. One of these, titled "Man the Producer," would be devoted to industrially manufactured products, including the automobile. The organizers invited Alfa Romeo to represent the entire industry by supplying an impressive concept car.

Alfa Romeo commissioned the Bertone design studio to implement this theme. There, the still-young Marcello Gandini designed a coupe body with unique details. These include the B-/C-pillar, which visually merged into one unit, and the double headlights half covered by a louvered grille. Striking air intakes behind the doors and a large, glass tailgate hinted at the drive concept Gandini had in mind: a mid-engine. Due to time constraints, however, the two prototypes finally sent to Canada were based on the standard components of the *Giulia* model, including its front-mounted engine.

The reaction of the visitors to Expo 67, up to 500,000 every day, was overwhelming. With each day of the six-month exhibition, Alfa Romeo received more inquiries about a purchasable version of the "*Montreal*" show car. And in fact, an order to that effect was issued to the development department. To lower production costs, the chassis remained largely the same as that of the *Giulia*.

Gandini's spectacular body design was also changed only in those details in which the concept car was not compatible with the requirements of series production or licensing for use on the road. For example, the air vents in the flanks, intended for a mid-engine design, were retained but now served to ventilate the cockpit. When the lights were switched on, the two slats were mechanically folded down to release the four lamps in accordance with regulations.

With the drivetrain, on the other hand, the engineers went all out. They developed a tamer version of the V-8 engine from the *Tipo 33* super sports car. To achieve a power delivery suitable for everyday use, engine displacement was increased from 2 to almost 2.6 liters. For its time, the V-8 produced an impressive 200 hp (147 kW) in the production version.

In spring 1970, the Alfa Romeo *Montreal* celebrated its public premiere at the International Motor Show in Geneva. Only 3,925 examples were built until 1977, in cooperation between the Alfa Romeo factory in Arese and the Carrozzeria Bertone. Today, we have the enthusiasm of the visitors to Expo 67 to thank for a coveted classic car.

An Expo 67 poster identifies the Alfa Romeo *Montreal* as man's highest inspiration in the field of the automobile.

KING WEDGE

At the end of the 1960s, there was only one body shape that was considered particularly avant-garde. Three design studios made pioneering contributions to this state of affairs.

The *Cuneo* concept car of 1968 came from Pininfarina designer Paolo Martin (*previous spread*). Giorgetto Giugiaro's approach to the subject, the *Iguana* (*right*), unveiled a year later, was not quite as radical.

What to do with the chassis of a super sports car that has already been built and is not selling as well as expected? Alfa Romeo came up with the brilliant idea of making the unused chassis of the *Tipo 33 Stradale* available to design studios close to the company so that they could build concept cars on them.

No fewer than two chassis ended up at Pininfarina, where two design teams immediately set to work. One was led by Leonardo Fioravanti. He was a fan of a rather feminine line with pronounced curves. It's no coincidence that his 33.2 coupe concept bears a strong resemblance to a previous Pininfarina design, the Ferrari 250 P. Both models shared the same body made of fiberglass-reinforced plastic, the strongly curved windscreen, and the folding headlights, down to the last detail. Pininfarina presented the show car at the 1969 Paris Motor Show.

Fioravanti's colleague Paolo Martin went in a completely different stylistic direction. For him, the wedge was king. He unveiled his P33 Roadster at the 1968 Turin Motor Show. The wedge shape, made possible by placing the engine behind the cockpit, was already there but broken up by curves. This was apparently not yet radical enough for Martin.

One advantage of the *Tipo 33* chassis was that the bodywork could easily be removed. And so, the designer went to work again and followed up three years later with the *Cuneo*. *Cuneo* is the Italian word for wedge. And that's exactly what the show car looks like—the minimalist body rises continuously from front to back. Exciting details are the battery of headlights embedded in the front, the tight windscreen, and the fins mounted on the edges of the rear fenders. The V-8 engine's intake funnels jut boldly out of the otherwise flat surface behind the cockpit.

Bertone was also in search of the ultimate wedge. Here, Marcello Gandini wielded the drawing pencil, opting for a coupe. But even his *Carabo* study, presented at the 1968 Paris Motor Show and actually ready to drive, was exceptionally low with a height of 39 inches (99 cm). The hood, which tapered toward the front, merged practically seamlessly into the windscreen. The doors opened spectacularly upward. The engine compartment and rear windows were covered with black plastic louvers. The headlights were also covered by slats that swiveled upward when the lights were switched on. The iridescent green body color was a tribute to the beetle that gave the car its name.

With the *Carabo*, Gandini designed one of the most influential concept cars of this era. Numerous stylistic elements were later adopted by various production sports cars. The so-called scissor doors, for example, reappeared in many Lamborghini models, the slats above the engine in the Lancia Stratos and the DeLorean DMC-12.

In 1969, Bertone designer Marcello Gandini relied on the visual effect of scissor doors on the *Carabo*. His show car was also based on the chassis of the Alfa Romeo *Tipo 33 Stradale*.

In 1976, Bertone unveiled another show car based on the Tipo 33. The *Navajo* looked like it had come from a science fiction movie.

bertone

The P33 show car was typical for Pininfarina, combining a basic wedge shape with complex curves. The centrally positioned headlights were a stylistic feature of designer Paolo Martin.

Eight years later, Bertone took on another *Tipo 33* chassis. Actually, the era of wedge-shaped concept cars was long gone. But Bertone took this concept to the extreme once again. His *Navajo*, presented at the 1976 Geneva Motor Show, looked like a space glider from the science fiction series *Star Wars*, which did not start until two years later.

But not everything was just for show. Unlike its predecessors, the *Navajo* incorporated the latest aerodynamic findings. This was evidenced by an adjustable front lip and huge rear spoiler. It directed the airstream in such a way that hot air was sucked out of the engine compartment behind the cockpit. The space-age body was made of plastic. Another highlight: the headlights didn't fold upward out of the hood, but sideways out of the fenders.

Bertone had also given more thought to the cockpit than before. By extending the wheelbase, the *Tipo 33* chassis offered the occupants a little more space. Instead of instruments, there was a central screen behind the single-spoke steering wheel, on which all important information was displayed.

Giorgetto Giugiaro's contribution to this series, his first for Alfa Romeo with his own studio Ital Design, seems almost shy by comparison. The *Iguana*, presented at the 1969 Turin Motor Show, looked ready for production. Compared to the competitors' concept cars, the *Iguana* featured a fairly traditional interior with a two-spoke steering wheel and a large instrument panel with analog gauges.

In fact, Giugiaro used some of the *Iguana*'s elements in later works, such as the Maserati Bora and DeLorean DMC-12, whose body, however, was really made of stainless steel. The outer skin of the *Iguana*, whose weight was only about 1,543 pounds (700 kg), was made of plastic—apart from the B-pillars and the longitudinal members of the roof—and was still painted to look like bare metal.

The five surviving concept cars based on the *Tipo 33*, unique witnesses to the history of the automobile and the creative power of the Italian *carrozzerias*, have a common home—the Alfa Romeo factory museum in the Milanese suburb of Arese.

Left: With the *Carabo*, Bertone anticipated design elements that were later found in the Lancia Stratos, among others. The *Prototipo Speciale Pininfarina* (*bottom left*), on the other hand, had similarities to the Ferrari 250.

HIDDEN QUALITIES

The revolutionary aspects of concept cars are often hidden in their technology. And then, trade fairs are not enough to justify their existence.

***Previous spread*: the *Proteo* show car unveiled at Geneva in 1991 was a design study and technology demonstrator in one. The individual headlights are taken from the Alfa Romeo GTV and Spider, and the all-wheel drive from the Alfa Romeo 164.**

Following the end of the *Alfetta GTV* (1986), Alfa Romeo no longer had a coupe in its model range. Three years later, Zagato showed that the demand was definitely there with its ES30 "Experimental Sportscar." So the company's design department—then under the direction of Walter de Silva—and the engineering staff were given the task of thinking about a successor. A concept car with the project name *Proteo* was to sound out what was feasible.

The engineers brought out the big guns. In search of optimal maneuverability, they shortened the chassis of an Alfa Romeo 164 to that of a two-seater and added a self-steering rear axle. In addition, the car had electronically controlled all-wheel drive with a self-locking Torsen differential in the rear axle. The tried-and-tested 3-liter V-6 gasoline engine with an increased output of 260 hp served as the power unit.

Their colleagues in design were determined not to be outdone. They designed a retractable glass roof that disappeared under the trunk lid. At that time, a coupe convertible was a revolution. Chief designer De Silva also opted for a pronounced wedge shape with three individual headlights and reduced *scudetto*.

Admittedly, the *Proteo* presented to the public at the 1991 Geneva Motor Show had not yet been developed to production maturity. But its technology and design lived on in the all-wheel-drive Viscomatic—for example, in the Alfa Romeo 164 Q4—as did its characteristic wedge shape with the single headlights in the GTV and Spider versions of the 916 series.

Alfa Romeo pursued a completely different idea with the *Nuvola* concept car. The idea was to revive the tradition of the legendary *carrozzerias* and design a vehicle whose chassis could be fitted with different bodies with little effort. The engineers developed a space-frame chassis with four-wheel drive and the 152.5-cubic-inch (2.5 liter) V-6 in the engine compartment, producing up to 300 hp.

The body and interior of the show car shown at the 1996 Paris Motor Show were created at the company's own *Centro Stile*. The team, headed by the German Wolfgang Egger and the Italian Filippo Perini, opted for a design influenced by historical elements. The long hood, radiator grille, and horizontal air intakes, the so-called *trilobo*, were reminiscent of Alfa Romeo sports cars from the 1930s or 1950s. Even the name *Nuvola* is a tribute to one of the greatest racing drivers in the history of the brand, Tazio Nuvolari. But *Nuvola* also means cloud, which is why the unique piece is painted in light blue metallic. This color would be adopted for future production models under the name *Nuvola*.

Alfa Romeo built on fresh ideas from the outside with the *Diva* concept car in 2006. The coupe, reminiscent of the legendary *Tipo 33* from the 1960s, was a coproduction of the *Centro Stile* with the Centre for Research and Development at Fiat and students of star designer Franco Sbarro. Underneath the body, which had scissor doors and a front end in the style of a Formula 1 car, was the modified chassis of an Alfa Romeo 159. For example, the V-6 gasoline engine, which produced around 290 hp, was now placed behind the cockpit. The *Diva* may not have made it into series production, but it served as a rolling test laboratory for production methods and future technologies such as an electronically adjustable chassis and LED headlights, among other things. And it was one of the eye-catchers at the *Concorso d'Eleganza* at the Villa d'Este on Lake Como.

Left: For the *Diva* show car (2006), the Centro Stile Alfa Romeo cooperated with students of star designer Franco Sbarro. It would not be converted into a production model any more than the *Nuvola* from 1996 (*bottom left*), a homage to racing driver Tazio Nuvolari.

THE FUTURE IS NOW

Sometimes concept cars are close to reality, but more often, they're not.

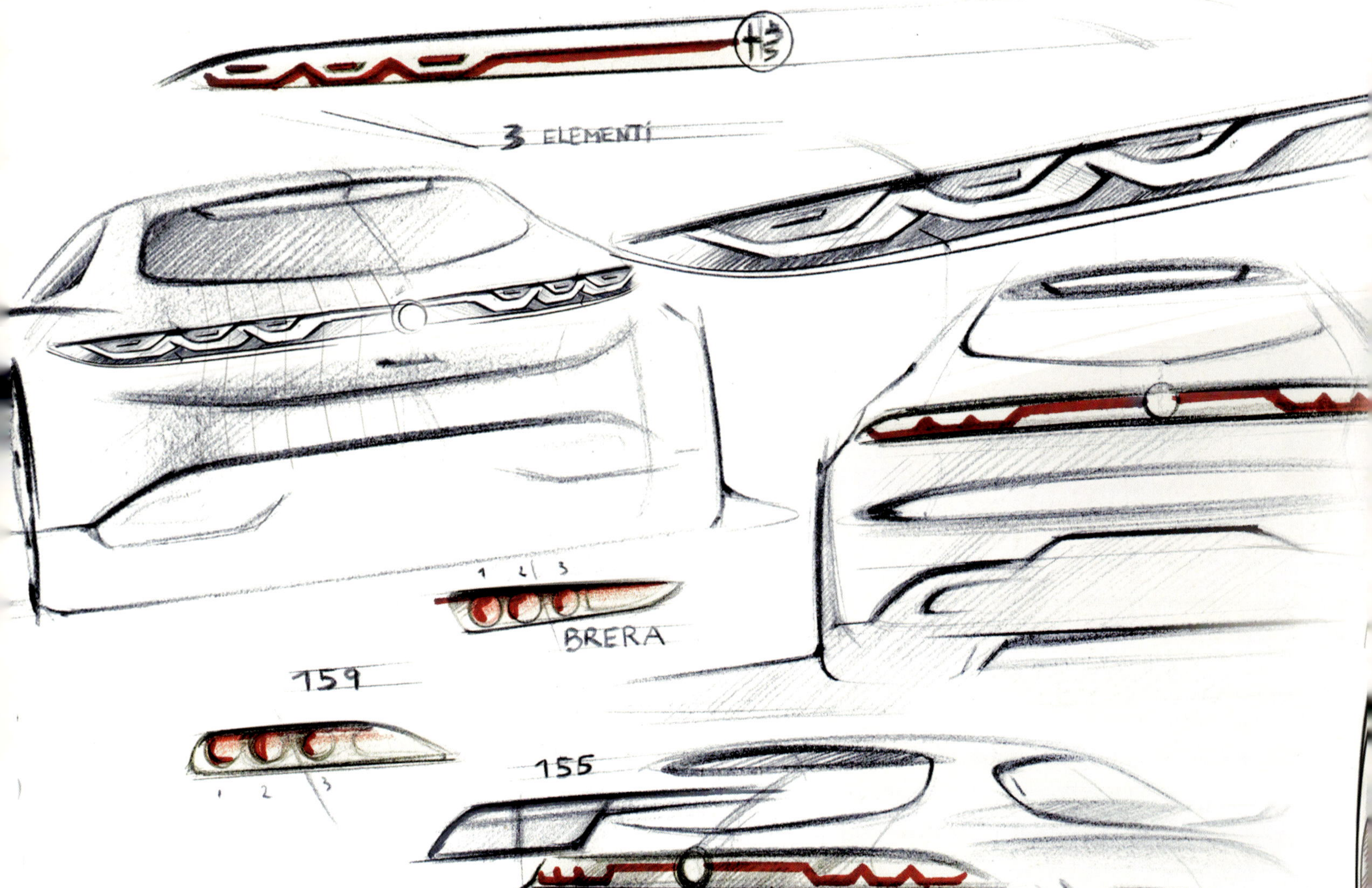

The *Tonale* concept car interpreted striking details of earlier Alfa Romeo models in a modern way. Unveiled in 2019, the study (*previous spread*) was practically ready for production.

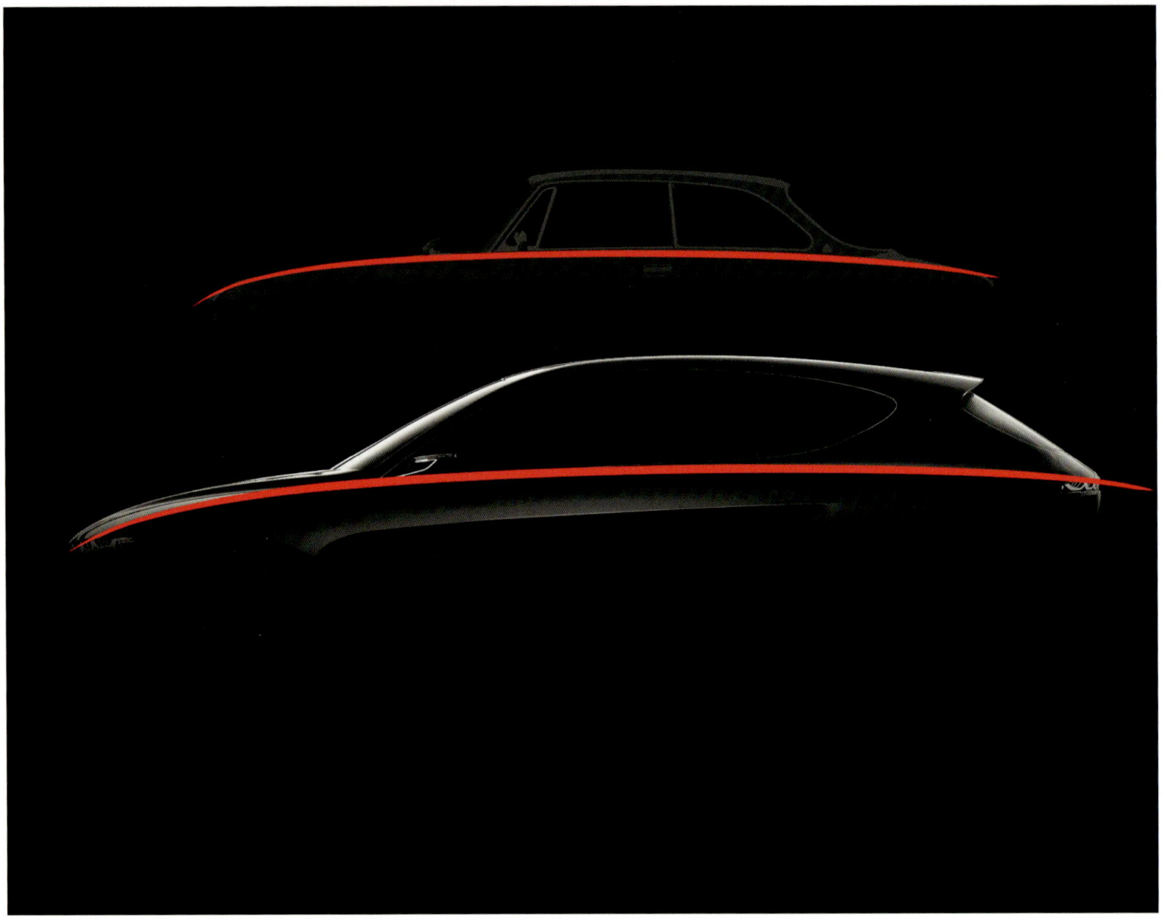

In profile, the *Tonale* concept car invoked the legendary Alfa Romeo *Giulia GTA* from the 1960s. Instead of a racing engine with two twin carburetors, a hybrid drive was envisaged for the *Tonale*.

Alfa Romeo and SUV? No one would have thought it possible until the 2003 Geneva Motor Show. But when the cloth was pulled off the *Kamal* concept car, even the biggest traditionalists had to admit to themselves: Why not?

After all, in Arabic *kamal* roughly means the synthesis of two completely opposite things. The SUV concept was based on the platform of the Alfa Romeo 159 and was not much more than a hint at this point—look, we could if we wanted to. That this was not an empty promise was shown fifteen years later by the *Stelvio*, which shares the platform with the current Giulia.

At about the same time, the term *kamal* was once again being bandied about in the trade press. But it quickly gave way to the new name *Tonale*, like *Stelvio* the Italian name for a pass in the Alps. The concept car of a compact SUV with this name, which was already very close to series production, was displayed by Alfa Romeo at the Geneva Motor Show in spring 2019.

The body design, which was the brainchild of Scott Krugger, evoked a number of elements deeply rooted in Alfa Romeo's great history. One example was the alloy wheels in the so-called dial design, which harken back to the iconic Tipo 33 Stradale from the 1960s. The striking vehicle flank is reminiscent of the two Spider models, the *Duetto* and the C52 *Disco Volante*. The classic GT silhouette of the *Tonale*, on the other hand, paid homage to the self-confident appearance of the Giulia GT Junior. The front of the Alfa Romeo *Tonale* featured the brand's signature *trilobo*, the triad of shield-shaped central grille and horizontal air intakes. The grille is flanked by headlights arranged in groups of three, evoking memories of the SZ and *Brera* coupes.

The *Tonale*'s interior was inspired by Alfa Romeo's racing tradition. The cockpit was consistently oriented toward the driver. The emotional touch was underlined by the choice of contrasting materials. For example, the coolness and hardness of aluminum were combined with the warmth of leather and Alcantara.

The *Tonale* displayed in Geneva in 2019 was already as good as ready for production, including electrified drive—which is more than can be said for the *Gloria* study shown six years earlier at the same venue. It was purely an exercise in style by the Centro Stile Alfa Romeo in collaboration with students from the European Design Institute in Turin. The racy coupe was intended to arouse the public's interest in the Alfa Romeo brand.

In other words, it fulfilled precisely the task that is in the specifications of every concept car.

Left: The *Gloria* show car, unveiled at the 2013 Geneva Auto Salon, was never intended to become a production car. Not so the *Kamal* (*below left*). This 2003 study was a very early forerunner of the Alfa Romeo *Stelvio*.

INDUSTRIAL REVOLUTION

The first Alfa Romeo was built in a small factory in the Milan suburb of Portello. Today, the brand has access to the ultra-modern factories of Stellantis N.V.

The first Alfa Romeo was [illegible] factory [illegible] suburb [illegible] Portello. [illegible] the brand has access to the [illegible] modern factories of [illegible]

A.L.F.A.'s first factory in the Milan suburb of Portello. In 1963 Alfa Romeo opened a new plant at Arese, where the *Giulia* was the first car to be produced (*previous spread*).

The owners of the *Società Anonima Lombarda Fabbrica Automobili* (Lombardy Automobile Manufacturing Company, or A.L.F.A.), the forerunner of Alfa Romeo founded in 1910, took a pragmatic approach. They needed a plant and a workforce for their planned production of automobiles, and they needed it fast. When the French brand Darracq went bankrupt, they seized the opportunity and took over its factory in the Milan suburb of Portello, including its 300 or so workers. The *Tipo 24 HP* designed by Giuseppe Merosi was the first A.L.F.A. to be manufactured here.

The conversion to military production brought about by the First World War, and the entry of investor Nicola Romeo allowed the young company to grow rapidly. In 1919, A.L.F.A. already employed around 2,200 people at its Portello plant, which had been expanded in the meantime. In the years after the war, the production of cars started up again. At the same time, however, tractors, commercial vehicles, and aero engines were also built in the factory.

With the outbreak of the Second World War, the Portello factory was again converted to produce military goods and was largely destroyed by bombing. After reconstruction, the factory reopened, producing household appliances in addition to automobiles. In 1950, there were around 5,000 people working at Portello.

Production was still largely manual and geared to small series of vehicles. This changed when Giuseppe Luraghi was commissioned by the state-owned Finmeccanica, Alfa Romeo's owner at the time, to completely restructure the company. With the 1900 and *Giulietta* models, the assembly line arrived at Portello. Series with low production volumes, such as the *Giulietta Sprint*, *Giulia Sprint,* and *Giulia Cabriolet*, were outsourced to specialized *carrozzerias* such as Bertone or Touring. At the same time, the production of commercial vehicles was transferred to a new plant at Pomigliano d'Arco in southern Italy.

By the early 1960s, the Portello plant had long been surrounded by residential areas, and an alternative was needed for further expansion. It was found on a large open space in neighboring Arese. The *Giulia* was the last model to be built entirely in Portello until 1965. After that, the ever-shrinking workforce exclusively produced prototypes or components such as engines. In 1986, after seventy-six years, the Portello plant was finally closed. The site and buildings were gradually repurposed or torn down by the city of Milan. The last building fell victim to the demolition crews in 2004.

Just one year later, Alfa Romeo also left its Arese plant, which had opened in 1963. In its heyday, around 19,000 employees worked here in the company's headquarters,

The Alfa Romeo 1900 (*left*) and the Alfa Romeo *Giulietta* (*below left*) were first produced on the assembly line at Portello. The peak workforce at the factory was 5,000 people.

Today, most Alfa Romeo production takes place at the FCA factory at Cassino in central Italy, where the most modern robots weld chassis and are responsible for transport.

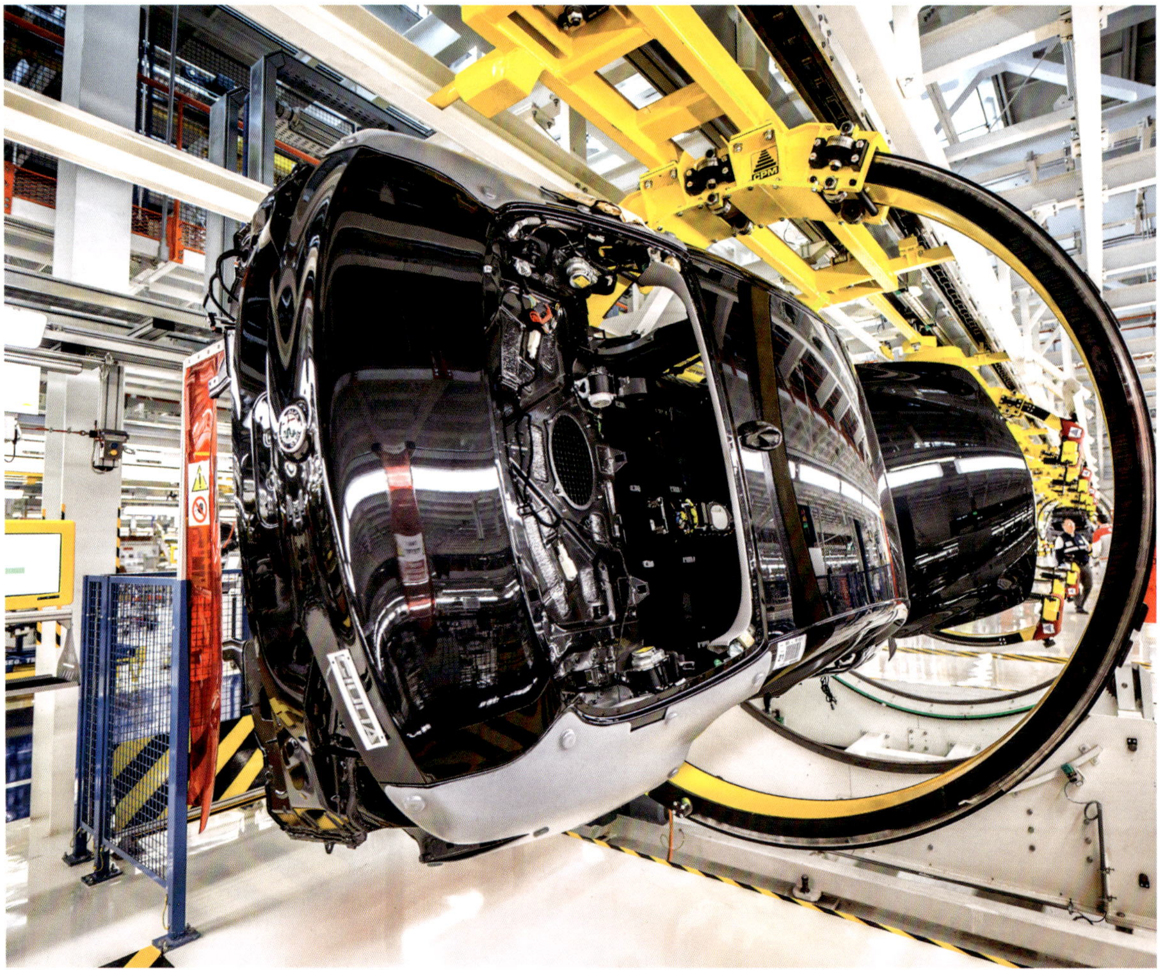

In 1963, Alfa Romeo opened a new factory at Arese; however, the cars gathered for a group photo in front of the new corporate headquarters included models that were not built there.

development, sales, design, and production of models such as the *Giulia*, *Alfetta*, *Giulietta*, 155, 164, and 916 series with GTV and *Spider*.

Due to the takeover by the Fiat Group, Alfa Romeo also had access to other plants and vice versa from 1986. While Alfa Romeo gradually shifted production to other plants, the Lancia Y10 and small series of the electrically powered Fiat *Seicento* and the Fiat *Multipla* with a natural gas engine, among others, were built at Arese. Alfa Romeo's last activities at Arese included the assembly of the V-6 engines and the design center.

In 2005, the plant closed its doors for good. Again, the existing buildings were demolished or sold to outside companies.

However, a small section remains for the factory museum, which has been open to visitors again since the summer of 2015 following a thorough renovation. Today, it offers a fantastic overview of the great history of Alfa Romeo at a site steeped in tradition.

Alfa Romeo has been producing commercial vehicles and aircraft engines at Pomigliano d'Arco near Naples since 1938. To further strengthen the economically weak south of Italy, Alfa Romeo also opened a completely new car factory at this location in 1972. Originally planned and built for the production of the *Alfasud*, the factory later also built the 33, 155, 145/146, 147/156, and 159 models. Since 2011, only the Fiat *Panda* has rolled off the production line at Pomigliano d'Arco.

Over the years, Alfa Romeo models have been built not only in its own factories but also at various Fiat and Fiat Chrysler Automobiles (FCA) plants, such as, for example, the 166 and the MiTo in Mirafiori/Turin. Alfa Romeo also uses external specialists for small series. The 916 series, for example, is built by Pininfarina, the RZ/SZ by Zagato, and the 8C and 4C super sports cars by Maserati in Modena.

More recently, the FCA plant in Cassino in central Italy has also come into focus. This is where the Alfa Romeo models *Giulietta* (since 2010), *Giulia* (since 2016), and *Stelvio* (since 2017) came off the production line. They are as far removed from the Tipo 24 HP of 1910 as the ultra-modern factory is from the original Alfa Romeo plant in Portello.

Cuore Sportivo
Driving with Passion

ALFA 155 SPORTING SUCCESSES HAVE A SOLID BASIS

The Alfa Romeo brand is inextricably linked to international racing—the experience of countless victories can be experienced in every Alta 155; sovereign power delivery from low speeds, high power reserves, fantastic lateral acceleration values, safe handling. And as in racing, safety is also the top priority in the active production version: independent sports suspension, internally ventilated disc brakes at the front, ABS standard on all Alfa 155 models. In addition, there is Alfa's typically rich equipment: central locking brakes, power steering, power windows at the front. The time is ripe for a new experience. Your Alfa Romeo dealer is waiting for you.

BUY ME!

Alfa Romeo's advertising style has changed frequently over 110 years. Let us take a short journey through the evolution of advertising in newspapers.

Max Hoffman, the US importer for Alfa Romeo, didn't attach much importance to artfully arranged photos in 1957—or on technical data. Instead, he made it clear that it was "more fun to drive a new Alfa Romeo," praised brakes developed in racing use, and made reference to the car's spacious trunk. Oh yes, he was also looking for dealers.

Alfa Romeo's advertising style has changed frequently over 110 years. Let us take a short journey through the evolution of advertising in newspapers.

No one had dreamed of television or the internet when the cornerstone of the Alfa Romeo brand was laid in 1910. Nor was there any talk of so-called testimonials. Accordingly, it was inconceivable that actresses such as Catherine Zeta-Jones (*The Mask of Zorro*) and Uma Thurman (*Kill Bill*) or the German actor Claus Theo Gärtner (*Ein Fall für Zwei*) would advertise for Alfa Romeo. It would have been easier to imagine a Formula 1 driver—at that time correctly called a Grand Prix driver—in this role. In this respect, Kimi Räikkönen would have sounded credible as ambassador for Alfa Romeo even back then. Apart from the fact that 110 years ago, there were no successful Grand Prix drivers from Finland.

The only form of advertising that has survived from the early years of Alfa Romeo into the twenty-first century is that in newspapers. Of course, printed advertising has also changed countless times over the decades along the currents of style and fashion. And so, advertisements are always also an expression of the zeitgeist of their respective epochs.

In the late 1930s, the Alfa Romeo 8C 2900 B was the brand's top model and, for mere mortals, unaffordable. In this respect, the ad—even though it was in two colors and had been stripped of all information—served primarily to cultivate the image.

In the mid-1960s, Alfa Romeo was proud of the *Giulia*, which it claimed was "designed by the wind." The exemplary drag coefficient was complemented by a "size that surprises you when you park" and an "interior that you appreciate only after driving a few hundred kilometers."

In the 1980s, consumers of magazines still had time to read advertisements carefully. Almost all the technical data for the Alfa Romeo 75 *America* (built between 1987 and 1990) is listed in this ad. The copywriter concludes, "Passion has never been stronger." The 1979 Alfa Romeo 6 is praised as the "Italian alternative." Technical data and a list of service features are also included.

This ad from 1980 would probably no longer be published today. In any case, the "wedge called *Giulietta*" exhibits a lean that might raise questions about the quality of its chassis. But perhaps the photo is deceptive. Because according to the text, the *Giulietta* "is master of the road at any speed and under all conditions."

Today, brand ambassadors, also known as testimonials, play an important role in advertising. Kimi Räikkönen, former Formula 1 World Champion, drove the Alfa Romeo *Stelvio* in several TV commercials beginning in 2019 (*above*). Catherine Zeta-Jones (*center*) said of the 1999 Alfa Romeo 156 Sportwagon, "I don't wear jewels; I drive them." And Uma Thurman (*below*) stated clearly about the 2010 launch of the Alfa Romeo *Giulietta*: "Without a heart, we'd all just be machines."

WHO INVENTED IT?

From dual ignition to common-rail direct injection and the carbon-fiber chassis, Alfa Romeo has been a trendsetter in innovative technologies for a century.

In the 1920s, only chassis-engine combinations were bought directly from Alfa Romeo. The engine of the Tipo 6C 1750, one of the first six-cylinder cars, was designed by Vittorio Jano.

In the early days of the automobile, a flash of inspiration was often all that was needed. At the end of the 1920s, when the engineers at Alfa Romeo were using supercharging to extract more and more power from the engine of the Tipo 6C 1500, the technology available at the time reached its limits in terms of the seal between the engine block and the cylinder head. The solution was as simple as it was ingenious: weld the block and head together, which in Italian was called *testa fissa* (fixed head). Where there is no seal, none can burn out. The disadvantages resulting from this construction in terms of assembly and maintenance were accepted for a racing engine.

The supercharger alone was an innovative technology for its time. The mechanically driven blower delivered additional air into the cylinders with overpressure. With more available oxygen, more fuel could be burned and more power could be generated per power stroke. The fact that fuel consumption rose to astronomical heights was of little interest to the racing team. The 1.5-liter, eight-cylinder engine with its two-stage supercharger installed in the Tipo 158 and 159 Formula 1 cars was capable of consuming up to 26.4 gallons (100 liters) per 62 miles (100 km)—but it rewarded Alfa Romeo with two world championship titles in 1950 and 1951.

The commitment to motorsport rubbed off on the technical side of Alfa Romeo's production cars. Until the 1950s, the Portello plant mainly built chassis without bodywork. There was usually a choice of different engine variants, but the normal customer could also order a racing power unit just like that. He then had the naked chassis fitted out by a *carrozzeria* (body maker) of his choice, depending on the car's intended use—everyday vehicle or race car. Without too much exaggeration, owners of an Alfa Romeo could be proud of driving a car that had won Grand Prix races, the *Mille Miglia* road race, and the 24 Hours of Le Mans.

The 1.5-liter, six-cylinder engine of the Tipo 6C 1500 was also trendsetting for Alfa Romeo technology in another respect—it had two overhead camshafts in the Sport variant. The version built from 1933 onward, which was enlarged to 116 cu. in. (1.9 liters), had a cylinder head made of aluminum for the first time, and even an engine block made of this light metal on an experimental basis.

When a four-cylinder was needed for the future *Giulietta* small family car in the early 1950s, the engineers did not hesitate to adopt overhead camshafts and an alloy cylinder head. Alfa Romeo thus offered technology that had been tried and tested in racing in the first large-scale production model in the brand's history. The potential of this "double cam" was demonstrated in 1966 by the *Giulia GTA*. It was a so-called homologation model (i.e., the production vehicle prescribed as the basis for racing cars in touring car races). The rules state that the engine must retain its

Racing technology in production cars has a long tradition at Alfa Romeo. In 1955, the Giulietta *Sprint* impressed with two overhead camshafts and a cylinder head made of light alloy.

ALFA ROMEO HAS BEEN MAKING RACING ENGINES WITH TWIN CAMSHAFTS AND DUAL IGNITION SINCE 1914.

basic structure. To optimize combustion, the technicians modified the cylinder head to accommodate two spark plugs per cylinder.

Alfa Romeo first used this technology in a Grand Prix racing car back in 1914. At the end of the 1960s and the beginning of the 1970s, the *Giulia GTA*—and the racing versions developed from it—racked up countless victories on the racetrack and won a whole series of titles in the European Touring Car Championship. And from 1986 onward, the twin ignition system, then called "Twin Spark," helped production models such as the 75, 145, 147, and 156 achieve sporty performance.

In the *Giulia GTA* era, Alfa Romeo also experimented with two other technologies that are now indispensable in production vehicles: supercharging and fuel injection. The *sovralimentato* (turbocharged) charging method introduced in the *Giulia GTA SA*, with the blower hydraulically driven by sump oil, was not technically convincing. The now-common turbocharger, which is driven by the exhaust gas flow, succeeded in doing so a little later. The SPICA injection system, on the other hand, had a long career at Alfa Romeo.

Once again, technology was transferred from the racetrack to the road. The mechanical fuel injection system developed by *Società Pompe Iniezione Cassani & Affini* (Cassani and Affini Injection Pumps, or SPICA) made the *Giulia GTAm* a successful racing car. In various Alfa Romeo production cars, the highly complex component is used above all to meet increasingly stringent exhaust regulations; for example, in the USA, which is no longer possible with carburetors.

The *Tipo 158* and *159* Grand Prix racing cars, with which Nino Farina and Juan Manuel Fangio became Formula F1 world champions in 1950 and 1951, respectively, had a

Alfa Romeo was the inventor of common-rail direct injection, internally called JTD or JTDm depending on the generation. Today, this technology has a virtual monopoly on turbodiesels.

special drivetrain design that allowed the weight to be distributed between the front and rear wheels. The gearbox and clutch were connected to the rear axle separately from the engine, which was positioned in front. Alfa Romeo also introduced this transaxle arrangement in the production car with a new mid-size sedan in 1972. The *Tipo 158* and *159* were nicknamed "*Alfetta*" (little Alfa) because of their small size compared to the prewar Grand Prix cars. So, it stands to reason that *Alfetta* was chosen as the model name for the new production sedan.

As usual, the *Alfetta* had a longitudinally mounted engine that powered the rear wheels via a driveshaft. But Alfa Romeo had been researching other drive concepts for several years. It was clear to the development department that the comparatively small vehicles needed in the future in the age of mass motorization would have to use the available space in a completely different way.

As early as 1960, a prototype with project number 103 was ready. Its transversely mounted gasoline engine with a capacity of 55 cubic inches (0.9 liters) at the front of the car transmitted power to the front wheels. The notchback body anticipated the *Giulia*, which was presented a little later with conventional rear-wheel drive. The technical findings, on the other hand, formed the basis for the *Alfasud*, which in 1972 helped start the trend toward front-wheel drive in small cars. At that time, no one would have guessed that in about twenty-five years Alfa Romeo would offer front-wheel drive even for large sedans and estate cars with engines producing in excess of 200 hp.

Even greater skepticism would probably have been reaped at that time by the prediction that in the not-too-distant future, Alfa Romeo would, at least temporarily, sell as many vehicles with diesel engines as with gasoline engines. Indeed, the commercial success—or rather failure—of the *Giulia Diesel*, built for just two years in 1976 and 1977, did not seem encouraging. However, the model, developed as a reaction to the oil crisis, had a rather crude diesel engine under the hood and had been designed for commercial vehicles. Scoffers spoke of the "slowest Alfa Romeo ever" in view of an eternity of forty-five seconds that passed when accelerating from zero to 62 mph (100 kph).

It was not until the beginning of the 1990s that the development department took up the subject of diesel with full commitment. In conjunction with turbochargers, diesel engines have since achieved remarkable performance. But the question of how to get the fuel into the cylinder with high precision and timing had not yet been solved perfectly. So-called pre-chamber diesels, in which auto-ignition was initialized outside the actual combustion chamber, were not an optimal solution.

Alfa Romeo was not alone in researching methods of injecting fuel directly into the combustion chamber. This requires very high pressure, beyond 14,503 psi (1,000 bar).

Left: The pump for SPICA mechanical petrol injection system. *Below left*: Transaxle principle—in the Alfa Romeo *Alfetta*, the gearbox and clutch are not located at the front next to the engine, but on the rear axle.

Project 103: Alfa Romeo began experimenting with front-wheel drive in 1960. The design of the prototype was reminiscent of the *Giulia*. The technology became production-ready in 1972 with the arrival of the *Alfasud*.

While competitors used one high-pressure pump per cylinder, Alfa Romeo's engineers opted for a common high-pressure accumulator for all cylinders. The system, known as common rail, has advantages; today, it works with pressures far beyond 29,000 psi (2,000 bar) and has practically replaced the pump-nozzle process, at least in the passenger car sector.

Alfa Romeo was the first car manufacturer in the world to use common rail direct injection under the designation JTD in the 156 model (from 1997). The Alfa Romeo 147 also benefited from this technology. Suddenly, diesel vehicles achieved driving performances on a par with, and sometimes even superior to, gasoline cars. And all this with significantly lower fuel consumption. Common rail technology is constantly being improved; for example, the injection process is divided into smaller portions. At Alfa Romeo, this generation is called JTDm. From here, it is only a small step until direct injection also finds its way into petrol engines, at Alfa Romeo under the abbreviation JTS.

Another technical revolution in the engine sector celebrated its world premiere in 2009 in the Alfa Romeo MiTo. The technology called MultiAir replaced—initially only for the intake valves—conventional mechanical valve actuation by a camshaft. With MultiAir, an electronically controlled hydraulic element was installed between the cam and the valve. The fully variable control meant not only that the throttle valve was needed only for emergency operation, but each valve could also be controlled individually and even opened several times per intake stroke. Both factors increased performance and reduced fuel consumption and exhaust emissions.

From 1999, the Alfa Romeo 156 was the first car in its segment to offer the Selespeed gearbox, which was all about increased driving pleasure. This was a conventional manual gearbox, but the gears were changed by hydraulic actuators rather than mechanically by the movement of a gearshift lever. Selespeed offered the comfort of an automatic without the power loss of a torque converter. Moreover, in addition to the fully automatic mode, the electronics provided the driver with the option of changing gears on demand. In the first version, buttons on the steering wheel were provided for this purpose, but paddle shifters quickly took their place.

Ten years later, Alfa Romeo refined the automated manual transmission into the TCT (Twin Clutch Transmission). In principle, this consisted of two gearboxes, one with the even gears and one with the odd gears, each with its own clutch. While the vehicle was moving in one gear, the next one was in the parallel clutch while the second one was closing. The transition is lightning fast. In the Alfa Romeo MiTo, *Giulietta*, and 4C, this allowed upshifts during acceleration with virtually no interruption in traction.

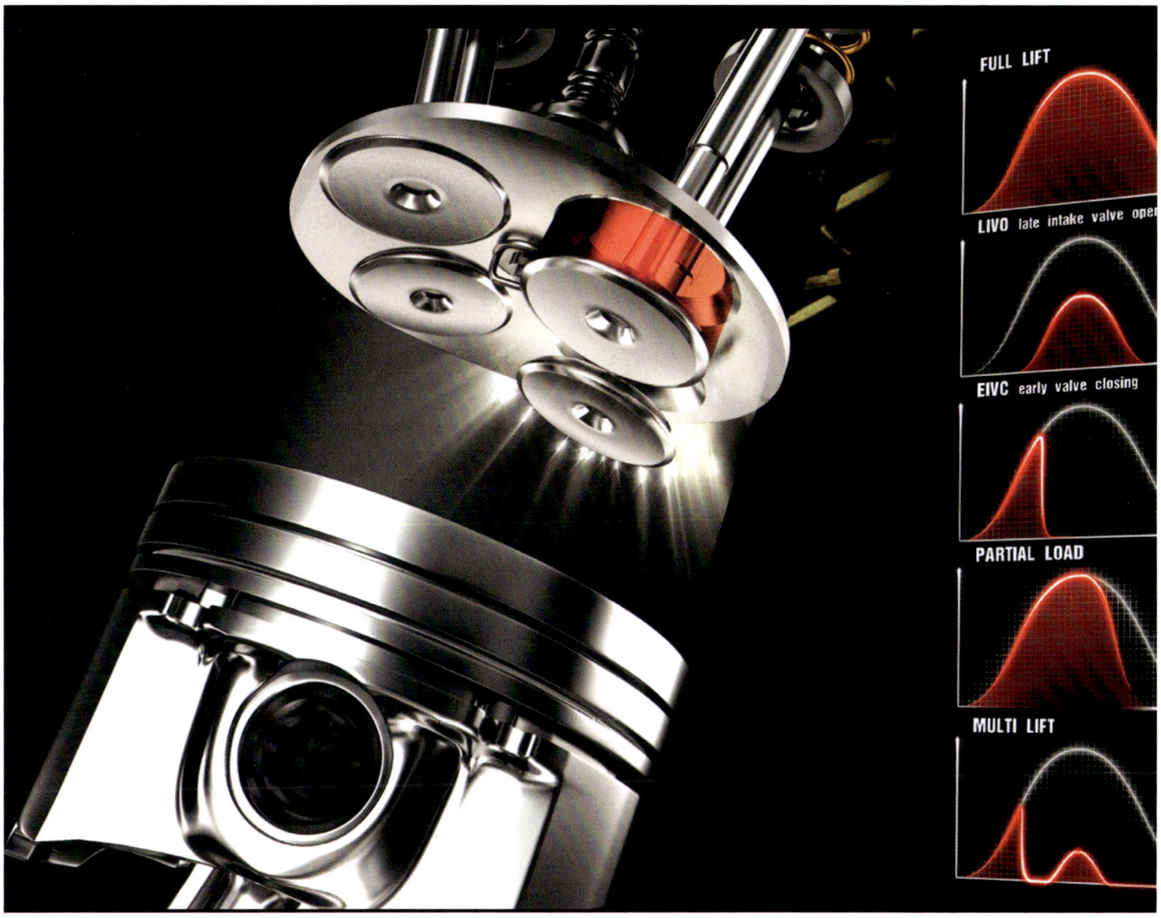

MultiAir technology makes possible electro-hydraulically controlled valves. This allows freely programmable opening and closing times, which optimizes efficiency.

THE DNA DRIVING PROGRAM SYSTEM MAKES POSSIBLE THE BALANCING ACT BETWEEN COMFORT AND SPORTINESS.

Because in the twenty-first century, everyday qualities are also expected from very sporty vehicles, Alfa Romeo developed the DNA system. Behind the abbreviation stood the possibility to change the character of a car in three stages via a toggle switch. The response of the steering, shock absorbers, and brakes, as well as the reactions of the engine to movements of the accelerator pedal, varied from the sporty "Dynamic" to the comfortable "Comfort" to "All Weather" for critical road conditions such as snow and ice. The *Quadrifoglio* versions of the Alfa Romeo *Stelvio* and *Giulia* also came with a fourth mode, "Race," which reduces the sensitivity of the electronic driver assistance programs and sharpens the exhaust sound for driving on a racetrack.

In the 4x4 versions of the Alfa Romeo *Stelvio*, the position of the DNA switch also influenced the effect of the Q4 four-wheel drive. Alfa Romeo first used the Q4 combination in 1992 on the 155 model with four-wheel drive. Through the 164, 156, and 159 models, four-wheel drive was further and further refined until it reached its current level in the *Stelvio* and *Giulia*. In both models, Q4 normally offered all the sporting advantages of rear-wheel drive. Only when road conditions required it did the electronically controlled Torsen center differential transfer up to 50 percent of the engine's torque to the front wheels for optimum traction.

The 4x4 system on the Alfa Romeo *Stelvio Quadrifoglio* went one step further. Its rear differential distributed the engine torque perfectly between the left and right rear wheels (Active Torque Vectoring). This effectively prevented the wheels from spinning during acceleration.

Thanks to Active Torque Vectoring, the Alfa Romeo *Giulia Quadrifoglio*, which was driven only by the rear wheels, also optimally converted its engine power into propulsion, even on roads with varying traction conditions. In addition, the top model in the *Giulia* range offered an electronically

The Alfa Romeo *Giulia* and *Stelvio* models (*photo on right*) are based on the Giorgio platform (chassis + engine + electronics), which allows rear-wheel and all-wheel drive.

adjustable spoiler lip under the front bumper (Active Front Splitter). The different speed-dependent positions varied the downforce generated at the front axle and ensured unwavering straight-line stability even at very high speeds.

In the *Giulia* and *Stelvio*–especially in the 510hp (375-kW) top models with the *Quadrifoglio* logo on the front fenders–Alfa Romeo relied heavily on carbon fiber to reduce weight. This high-tech material was used, for example, for the driveshaft and, depending on the model version, also for the fenders, hood, roof, and seat shells.

The use of carbon fiber was taken to the extreme in the Alfa Romeo 4C (from 2013). This compact super sports car was based on a monocoque chassis baked entirely from carbon fiber. The body was made of plastic, and the subframe for the engine positioned behind the cockpit was made of aluminum. The result of this extremely lightweight construction was a weight of less than 1,984 pounds (900 kg).

The Alfa Romeo 6C 1500 from 1927 weighed about the same. However, this figure included only the pressed steel chassis, including the drivetrain, without the body.

The carbon fiber monocoque of the Alfa Romeo 4C (*bottom left*) roughly weighs just 143 pounds (65 kg). Nevertheless, it is extremely torsion-resistant and offers a high degree of accident safety.

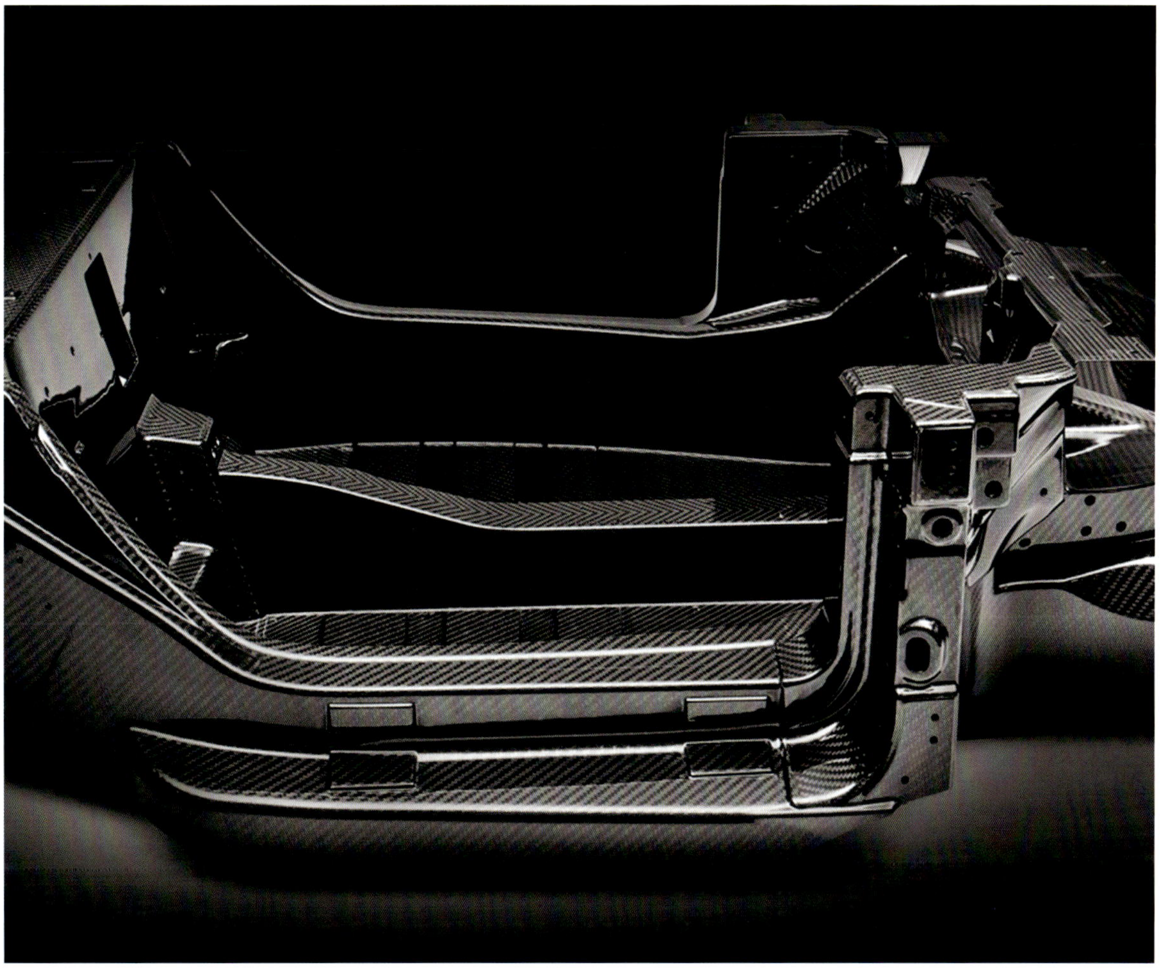

THE TIME MACHINE

A visit to the Alfa Romeo factory museum in the Milan suburb of Arese is like a trip through the brand's 110-year history.

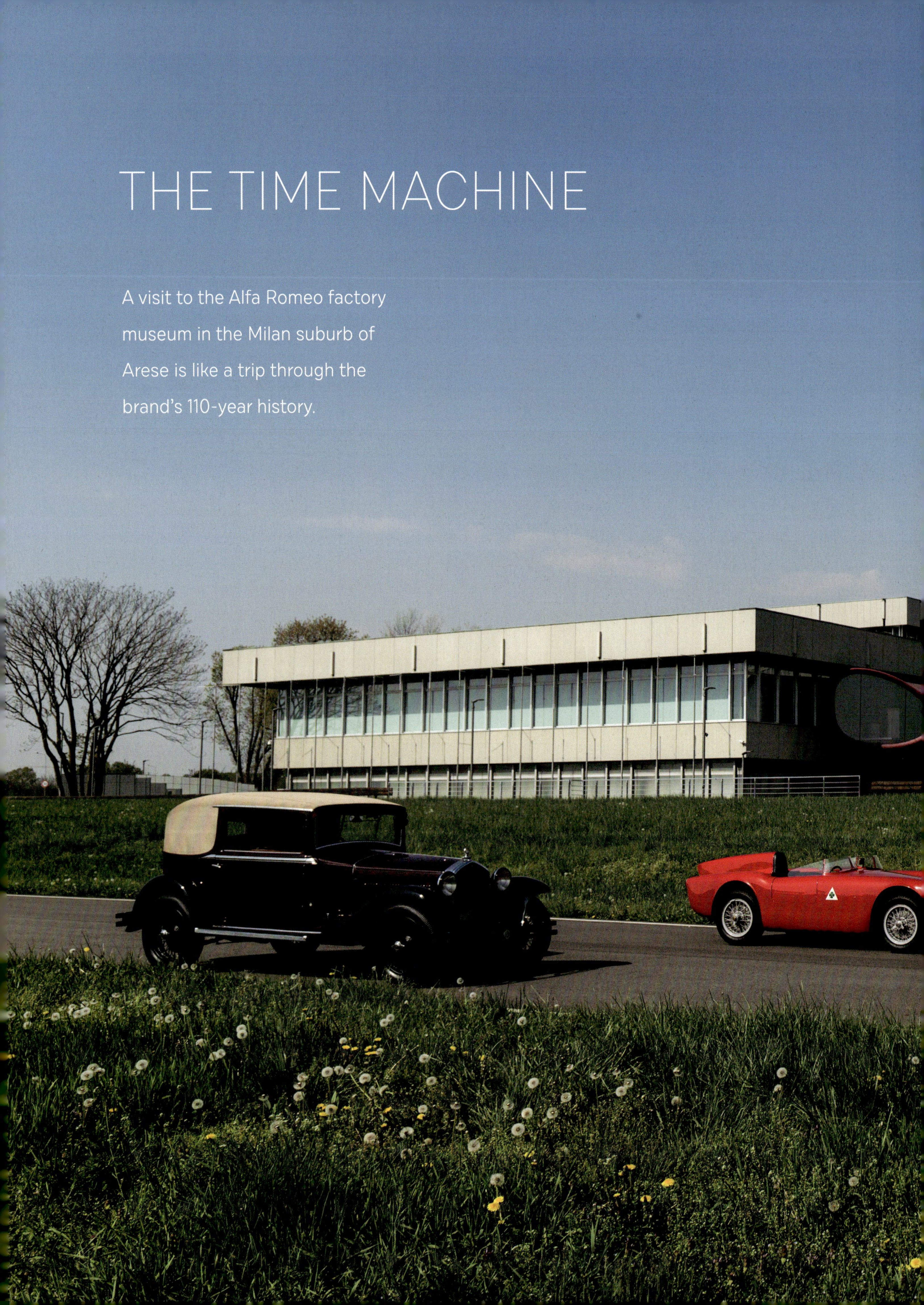

Alfa Romeo
MotorVillage
ARESE

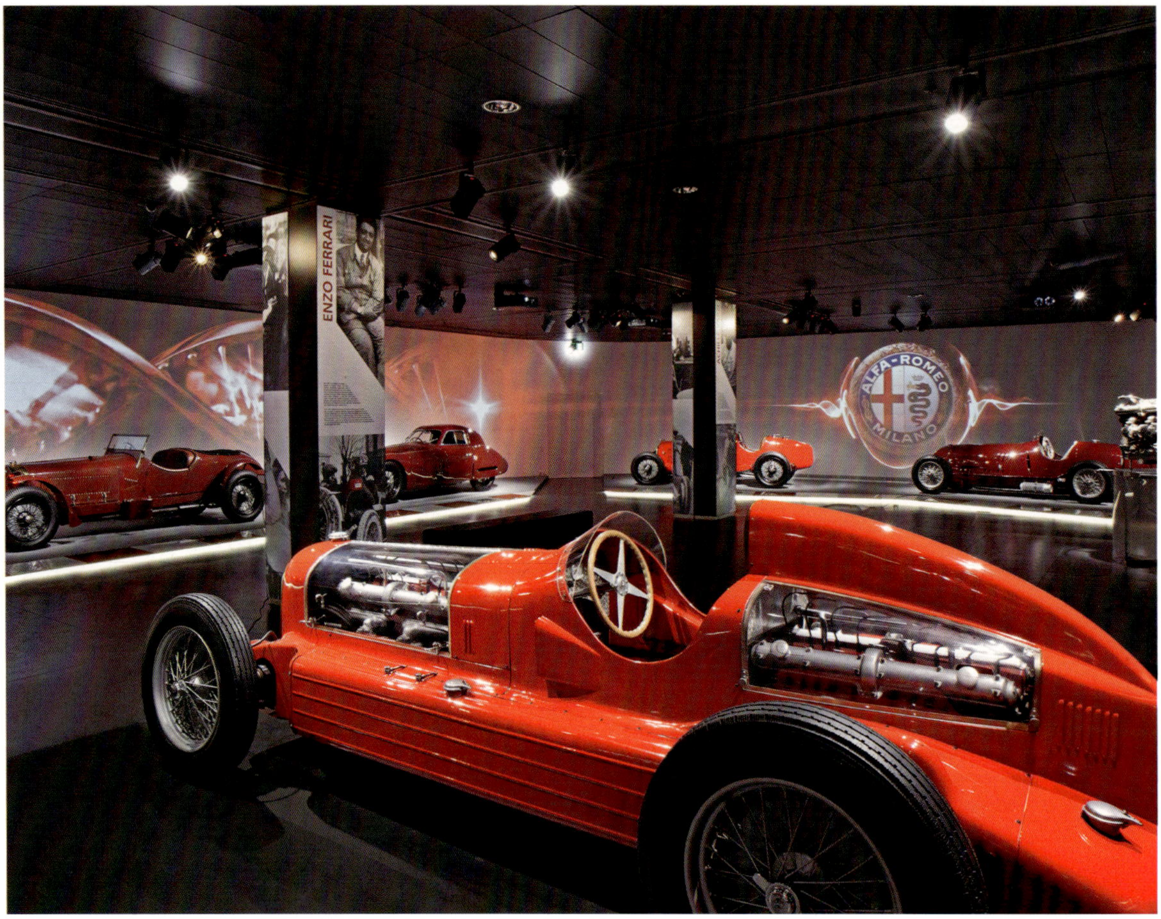

Alfa Romeo's racing cars are on display In the "Speed" section. A highlight is the Tipo 16C *Bimotore* from 1935, equipped with two engines and built only twice.

Stepping through the front door, one feels as if one is in a time machine. The Alfa Romeo Museum—whose subtitle is "*La Macchina del Tempo*" (The Time Machine)—located on the former factory premises in the Milan suburb of Arese, takes visitors on a journey through the history of the brand, which began in 1910. It leads from the Tipo 24HP, the first automobile made by the *Società Anonima Lombarda Fabbrica Automobili* (Lombardy Automobile Manufacturing Company, or A.L.F.A.), through countless exhibits to Alfa Romeo's current involvement in the Formula 1 World Championship.

In the 1950s, Orazio Satta Puliga, then the director of Alfa Romeo, laid the cornerstone of the museum. The collection finally took shape under the direction of designer and historian Luigi Fusi. On December 18, 1976, the time had come—the museum was officially inaugurated in a management building that had been specially redesigned for this purpose. After the cessation of production and the relocation of the company headquarters, the museum had to be closed temporarily in 2009.

Renowned Italian architect Benedetto Camerana was finally commissioned to renovate the entire complex in line with Alfa Romeo's new direction, while at the same time bringing the substance of the historic building back to life. On June 24, 2015, the *Museo Storico Alfa Romeo* was ceremoniously reopened. Since then, fans of the brand have been able to take a journey into the automotive past in the "*Macchina del Tempo*." They have also visited the bookshop, café, and adjoining Motor Village in the brand center or taken part in events. Occasionally, visitors can also take their own Alfa Romeo for a spin on the in-house test track.

The entire layout of the museum building reflects the DNA of Alfa Romeo. The exhibitions include the most important production cars, design studies, prototypes, and racing cars of the brand founded in 1910. They not only illustrate the development of Alfa Romeo but also show a cross-section of the entire history of the automobile.

On six levels with a total area of 51,667 square feet (4,800 square meters), the *Museo Storico Alfa Romeo* displays about a quarter of the 250 cars in its collection. The exhibition is divided into three sections. On the ground floor, the "*Bellezza*" area deals with the interaction of style and design. Cars such as the Alfa Romeo *Giulia* of the 1960s were the symbol of a modern, educated, and mobile Italian society whose aspirations were for the *dolce vita* (the sweet life), not commercial success for its own sake. Another segment is devoted to "Alfa Romeo in the movies," others to the "Alfa Romeo *Giulietta* phenomenon" and the chapter "Alfa Romeo *Giulia*—design created by the wind."

The Museo Storico's vast archive preserves priceless documents from Alfa Romeo's past. It is accessible only on special occasions.

The Alfa Romeo Museum's collection is made up of more than 250 vehicles. They are not all on public display, and the spares wait in the large storage halls.

Located on the first floor, "Timeline" stands for the industrial development of Alfa Romeo, and almost every exhibit is accompanied by a multimedia presentation. The installation titled "Quelli dell'Alfa Romeo" describes how the brand became a legend within a hundred years and illustrates the decisive role played by thousands of workers, mechanics, designers, engineers, and managers.

The basement houses the "Speed" section, perhaps the most exciting and thrilling section for many Alfa Romeo fans. Here, visitors can take a look at the brand's unique racing history with the help of state-of-the-art multimedia presentations. Legendary racing cars such as the Tipo 6C 1750 *Gran Sport*, with which Tazio Nuvolari won the famous Mille Miglia long-distance race in 1930, the Tipo 159 *Alfetta*, which carried Juan Manuel Fangio to the Formula 1 World Championship in 1951, and the Tipo 33TT12, with which Alfa Romeo won the title in the Sports Car World Championship in 1975, are on display. As a highlight, the "Hall of Victories" awaits the visitors. Thanks to elaborately presented photos, films, and audio documents, they are almost live at the ten greatest victories by Alfa Romeo.

Only on special occasions are the documentation department and the huge warehouse open to the public. The parts of the collection that cannot be seen in the museum are kept on two floors. This treasure trove contains, among other things, another 150 vehicles; dozens of automobile, aircraft, and ship engines; hundreds of models; trophies; works of art and accessories; and even a racing motorboat.

The exhibits stored here, which are not part of the museum's permanent collection, represent an exceptional reserve. The museum uses them for themed temporary exhibitions, for example. They are also a unique opportunity for Alfa Romeo to participate in external events and exhibitions of all kinds.

Alfa Romeo Factory Museum "La Macchina del Tempo"

Viale Alfa Romeo, 20200 Arese (near Milan).

Information, opening hours, etc.:

www.museoalfaromeo.com

Left: This presentation illustrates the versatility of the Alfa Romeo *Giulia*. *Below left*: Concept cars have their own area. At left is the *Carabo* from 1968; at right, the “Teardrop Car” from 1914.

Racing Since 1910

Alfa Romeo has been active in motor sport for more than a hundred years. Its palette of victories ranges from the Mille Miglia to the Formula 1 World Championship.

The *Tipo RL*, which won the 1923 *Targa Florio*, was the first Alfa Romeo racing car to wear the *Quadrifoglio* emblem on its hood. The four-leaf clover was a lucky charm for works driver Ugo Sivocci.

THE BEGINNING

Early on, Alfa Romeo relied on the advertising power of racing. In 1923 Alfa Romeo achieved its first major win in the Targa Florio road race.

The automobile had only just been invented when the first races were organized. Starting in 1911, the newly founded *Anonima Lombarda Fabbricca Automobile*, from which Alfa Romeo emerged a decade later, was involved in racing. Probably no other brand can point to such a long and successful tradition in motorsport.

Alfa Romeo achieved its first successes with specially prepared versions of the Tipo 24HP. Giuseppe Merosi, head of the design office, also developed a car for Grand Prix races, which in 1950 became Formula 1. Merosi opted for a four-cylinder engine with a capacity of almost 275 cubic inches (4.5 liters). But the First World War, which broke out in 1914, put a stop to the project.

A new era dawned for Alfa Romeo in 1922 with the Tipo RL. Now, the brand's sportiest models were powered by six-cylinder engines. Of course, Alfa Romeo also planned to enter the Targa Florio. The most important road race in Europe at the time was the brainchild of Sicilian businessman Vincenzo Florio. For the winner, he offered an honorary prize in the form of a bronze plaque (Italian: *targa*), which gives the event its name.

The route and length of the course varied from year to year, at times reaching almost 620 miles (1,000 km). In 1923, it consisted of four laps of a 67-mile (108km) loop with the start and finish in Cerda.

In 1914, Alfa Romeo was preparing for Grand Prix racing. Designer Giuseppe Merosi himself took the wheel for test drives. The First World War prevented the racing car from being used, however.

THE GRAND PRIX RACE CAR HAD AN ENGINE WITH TWO OVERHEAD CAMSHAFTS AND DUAL IGNITION.

Alfa Romeo sent four RLs on the Tour of Sicily. Two of them had an 88hp 183-cubic-inch (3.0-liter) engine under the hood. Two other vehicles were given a larger six-cylinder engine with just under 195 cubic inches (3.2 liters) and 7 more horsepower. The drivers were the young Enzo Ferrari, his mentor Ugo Sivocci, plus Antonio Ascari and Giuseppe Campari.

As was customary in that era, the starting numbers were raffled off. To his horror, the highly superstitious Sivocci drew number 13. To prevent him from seriously considering leaving, the Alfa Romeo mechanics painted a four-leaf clover on the car's hood for good luck. With a heavy heart, Sivocci drove to the starting line with his teammates.

Ascari crossed the finish line in the 183-cubic-inch (3.0-liter) RL with the fastest time after around 268.4 exhausting miles (432 km) on unpaved roads and more than seven hours. But because he had taken two helpers on board after an electrical problem shortly before, the stewards demanded that he drive back to where the repair had taken place, and officially finish the race without passengers.

As Ascari was making his second attempt, he was overtaken by teammate Sivocci, who was driving one of the RLs with a 3.2-liter, six-cylinder engine. Sivocci and mechanic/co-driver Angelo Fugazza gave Alfa Romeo its first victory in the Targa Florio victory, which it had

Right: Ugo Sivocci and mechanic in the Alfa Romeo RL on their way to victory in the 1923 *Mille Miglia*. The four-leaf clover is a reference to the four factory drivers Sivocci, Antonio Ascari, Giuseppe Campari, and Enzo Ferrari. After Sivocci's death the white background was changed to a triangle.

In the 1920s, Enzo Ferrari was a factory driver for Alfa Romeo. He created Scuderia Ferrari and focused on development of the factory Alfa race cars and ultimately took full control of its racing division. In 1947, he established his own sports car brand.

been chasing since 1911. Ascari finished second, almost three minutes behind.

Since then, Sivocci's lucky charm, the *Quadrifoglio Verde* (four-leaf clover), has adorned all of Alfa Romeo's racing cars, and more recntly also the brand's sportiest production cars. The white square that originally served as the background–symbolic of the four factory drivers–was replaced by a triangle when Sivocci was killed in an accident during practice for the 1923 Italian Grand Prix.

The youngest of the remaining trio of works drivers was Enzo Ferrari. The son of a metalworker from Modena, he eventually took part in forty-seven races for Alfa Romeo, winning over a dozen of them. In 1929, he founded his own racing team in Modena, which, as Scuderia Ferrari, contested the factory races for Alfa Romeo until 1933 and then used the racing cars from Milan privately. When Alfa Romeo was officially allowed to resume motor racing in 1937, Ferrari became director of the Alfa Corse works team. In 1939 they parted company, not entirely by mutual agreement. From 1947 onward, Ferrari sold sports cars under his own name, which over the years made him a legend.

In 1950, Ferrari's racing division, which had moved to Maranello, met Alfa Romeo in Formula 1, the world champion that year and the following year. When José Froilán González scored the first victory for Ferrari at the 1951 British Grand Prix against the Alfa Romeo factory team, Ferrari is reported to have said in tears, "Today I killed my mother."

A characteristic feature of the Alfa Romeo 6C 1750 *Gran Sport* was its three headlights, sometimes with red covers. In the racing version, the cylinder head was welded to the block (*testa fissa*, or fixed head). The engine produced about 102 hp.

1,000 MILES AND MORE

The races became longer. Alfa Romeo won the Mille Miglia and the 24-hour race at Le Mans.

Brescia, just a few miles from Lake Garda, is actually the cradle of Italian Grand Prix racing. The first Italian Grand Prix was held in this industrial city in 1921. The disappointment was all the greater when the country's most important race was moved to Monza just one year later. Four young men were determined not to let this disgrace stand. Franco Mazzotti, Count Aymo Maggi, Giovanni Canestrini, and Renzo Castagneto envisioned a road race along the lines of the *Targa Florio*. With a route from Brescia to the capital Rome and back, they achieved a distance of 1,628 kilometers, almost exactly 1,000 miles. The *Mille Miglia* was born.

Alfa Romeo was already at the start at the premiere in 1927, with works driver Gastone Brilli-Peri even leading at times. But it wasn't until a year later that its time had come. Grand Prix star Giuseppe Campari and co-driver Giulio Ramponi won the race in the Tipo 6C 1500 Super Sport. Its six-cylinder engine produced 84 hp thanks to supercharging. Campari and Ramponi needed just over nineteen hours to cover the 1,000 miles–nonstop on largely unpaved roads.

Campari repeated the victory in 1929 in the Alfa Romeo 6C 1750. In the meantime, the *Mille Miglia* had become the toughest road race of its time. By 1930, this challenging race attracted 135 participants. Alfa Romeo factory drivers Achille Varzi and Tazio Nuvolari dueled for victory in their

Left: In 1930 Grand Prix star Tazio Nuvolari and his mechanic Battista Guidotti won the *Mille Miglia* in the Alfa Romeo 6C 1750. Two years earlier, Giuseppe Campari and co-driver Giulio Ramponi won in the *Tipo 6C 1500* (*below*).

Grand Prix drivers Achille Varzi (*left*) and Tazi Nuvoloni were friends, at least until Nuvolari stole victory from his Alfa Romeo factory teammate in the 1930 *Mille Miglia*.

ALFA ROMEO WON THE 24-HOUR RACE AT LE MANS FOUR TIMES IN A ROW FROM 1931 TO 1934.

6C 1750 *Gran Sport* racers. Varzi led until shortly before the finish, then Nuvolari overtook him in the dark–according to legend with his headlights off. For the first time, the average speed was over 62 mph (100 kph).

In 1932, the race started early in the morning instead of in the evening. Baconino Borzacchini won in the new Alfa Romeo 8C 2300. In 1933 it was Nuvolari's turn again, also in the 8C 2300, now driven by Scuderia Ferrari. In 1934, Nuvolari in the 8C 2300 and Varzi in the 8C 2600 again dueled over the entire distance. In the pouring rain, Varzi's Pirelli tires, developed specifically for these conditions, finally tipped the scales.

One year later, Scuderia Ferrari conjured up a two-seat version of the Alfa Romeo P3 Grand Prix racer. Carlo Pintacuda won with the prototype. He repeated this coup in 1937, this time in the 8C 2900A. Antonio Brivio won in the same model in 1936. In 1938, Clemente Biondetti in the Alfa 8C 2900B Touring Spider increased the winner's average speed to over 84 mph (135 kph). He finished with the last of Alfa Romeo's ten *Mille Miglia* victories before the outbreak of the Second World War.

The marque won again in 1947, making it forever the record winner of the race, which was held for the last time in 1957.

The racing cars used in Grand Prix or even the *Mille Miglia* were already becoming increasingly specialized by the 1920s, moving further and further away from production cars. This gave the top management of the French *Automobile Club de l'Ouest* (ACO) the idea of creating a 24-hour race for production cars. A 10.6-mile (17km) road course, the *Circuit de la Sarthe*, was chosen as the track.

At the premiere in 1923, thirty-five participants were on the grid. In 1931, Alfa Romeo entered a team for the first time. The engineers built a four-seat long version of the Alfa Romeo 8C 2300 especially for the Le Mans regulations.

The Alfa Romeo 8C 2300, built for endurance racing, was descended from the P2 Grand Prix car. Its eight-cylinder engine was equipped with two superchargers and produced up to 180 hp.

The original car with its short wheelbase had already won the *Mille Miglia* and the Italian Grand Prix at Monza.

The car's engine was an eight-cylinder that designer Vittorio Jano developed from the 122-cubic-inch (2-liter) power unit of the P2 Grand Prix car. The 140 cubic inches (2.3 liters) of displacement was distributed over two interconnected four-cylinder blocks made of light metal. A Roots supercharger ensured optimum charging of the combustion chambers with fuel-air mixture. The power output was 155 hp.

In June 1931, three 8C 2300s competed at Le Mans. The two factory cars had to concede defeat to the British team of Henry Birkin and Lord Howe, who had previously driven for Bentley. They reached an average speed of 77.7 mph (125 kph)—an almost unbelievable value for the time. The official Alfa Romeo drivers also lost out in 1932. Raymond Sommer (France) and Luigi Chinetti (Italy) finished ahead of factory drivers Franco Cortese and Giovanni Battista Guidotti (both Italian). Interestingly, Chinetti dropped out after his first shift on account of illness, after which Sommer sat behind the wheel for more than twenty hours.

The following year, four-seaters were no longer mandatory at Le Mans. Alfa Romeo therefore relied on the *Mille Miglia*-proven chassis variant with a short wheelbase and just two seats. And this time, the factory team did not let private drivers take the butter off its bread. Raymond Sommer and Tazio Nuvolari (Italy) finished just ten seconds ahead of their teammates Luigi Chinetti and Philippe de Gunsburg (France).

British drivers Brian E. Lewis and Tim Rose-Richards finished third, ensuring a flawless Alfa Romeo podium. In 1934, the brand took its fourth consecutive Le Mans victory. Chinetti and Philippe Etancelin (France) were superior in the 8C 2300, now with a 180 hp engine. Their lead over the runners-up after twenty-four hours: 112 miles (180 km).

Alfa Romeo entered an aerodynamically optimized version of the P3 in the 1934 Grand Prix at the AVUS motor racing circuit in Berlin. The French driver Guy Moll emerged victorious over the powerful German competition.

VITTORIO'S MIRACLE CAR

At the turn of the twentieth century, races held on public roads over long distances–from Paris to Madrid, for example–were the order of the day. However, serious accidents occurred more and more frequently. At the Gordon Bennett Cup in Ireland in 1903, a circuit with closed roads was therefore tried out. The system worked, and three years later the Automobile Club of France called such a race the Grand Prix for the first time.

In 1925, the time seemed ripe for the first World Automobile Championship; it consisted of four Grand Prix races, one in the USA and three in Europe. Alfa Romeo entered the Tipo P2, a development by Vittorio Jano. The engineer designed the brand's first in-line eight-cylinder engine under great secrecy. The 122-cubic-inch (2-liter) engine with its two-stage Roots supercharger initially produced 140 hp. The competition premiere in June 1924 at a 200-mile race in Cremona (Italy) was won by the Italian Antonio Ascari. He was measured at 121 mph (195 kph) on the straight–a world record. Two months later, the P2 started in a Grand Prix for the first time. At the French Grand Prix in Lyon, which covered more than 497 miles (800 km), victory went to Giuseppe Campari.

Jano revised the P2 for the 1925 World Championship. A new fuel–the ethanol-benzene mixture Elcosine–and a second carburetor increased power to 154 hp. Because the mechanic/co-pilot, which had been common until

Left: In 1925, Alfa Romeo won the first ever World Automobile Racing Championship with the *Tipo P2*. Gastone Brilli-Peri's victory in the Italian Grand Prix (*below*) was decisive.

EN VENTE ICI

The drivers who drove for Scuderia Ferrari (the Ferrari racing team that drove for Alfa Romeo)–hence the emblem on the Alfa Romeo P3–in 1934 included Achille Varzi, Louis Chiron, and Carlo Felice Trossi. That season the *Tipo P3* won eighteen Grand Prix races.

then, was banned from 1925, Jano used the space freed up in the cockpit for an additional fuel tank.

The Alfa Romeo factory team with the three Italian drivers Antonio Ascari, Giuseppe Campari, and Gastone Brilli-Peri skipped the season opener at the Indianapolis 500 (USA). At the Belgian Grand Prix in Spa-Francorchamps, Ascari won with a twenty-two-minute lead over Campari. At Monthléry (France), Ascari had a fatal accident; while in the lead, he overturned on a rain-soaked track. Nicola Romeo took the entire team out of the race. Brilli-Peri won the season finale at Monza (Italy). This secured the first world championship in the history of the automobile for Alfa Romeo. The brand was unable to defend the title –in the years that followed, only European championships were held.

With eighteen victories in major international races, the Alfa Romeo P2 was a model of success. But with its successor, the P3, engineer Vittorio Jano raised the bar even higher. Because Grand Prix racing now demanded more than 122 cubic inches (2 liters) of displacement, he designed a completely new in-line eight-cylinder engine. Displacement was initially 158.7 cubic inches (2.6 liters) but increased to 232 cubic inches (3.8 liters) by 1935. With the assistance of a Roots two-stage supercharger, the engine initially delivered 215 hp, and later 330 hp.

With a total of forty-six victories in major races, the Alfa Romeo P3 was the most successful racing car of its era. Its debut (GP Italy 1932 in Monza) ended with first place for the Italian driver Tazio Nuvolari. At a Grand Prix race in 1934 on the AVUS high-speed circuit in Berlin, the Algerian-born Frenchman Guy Moll won in an aerodynamically clad P3 with a larger 195-cubic inch (3.2-liter) engine. Nuvolari's most memorable victory came at the 1935 German Grand Prix at the Nürburgring against supposedly superior domestic competition from Mercedes and Auto-Union.

The "Flying Mantuan," as Nuvolari was known, became a legend in his lifetime and is today considered one of the best racing drivers of all time. Before his career in automobile racing, he became European champion on a motorcycle. For Alfa Romeo, he won competitions as diverse as the *Mille Miglia* and the 24-hour race at Le Mans and also won the European Grand Prix title in 1932.

Due to injuries, Nuvolari was forced to take several long breaks. He took these setbacks with a good dose of black humor. On his way to the *Targa Florio* on the Mediterranean island of Sicily, he is said to have once said to Alfa Romeo race director Enzo Ferrari, "I hope you didn't spend any money on my return trip. After all, maybe I'll be coming back in a coffin."

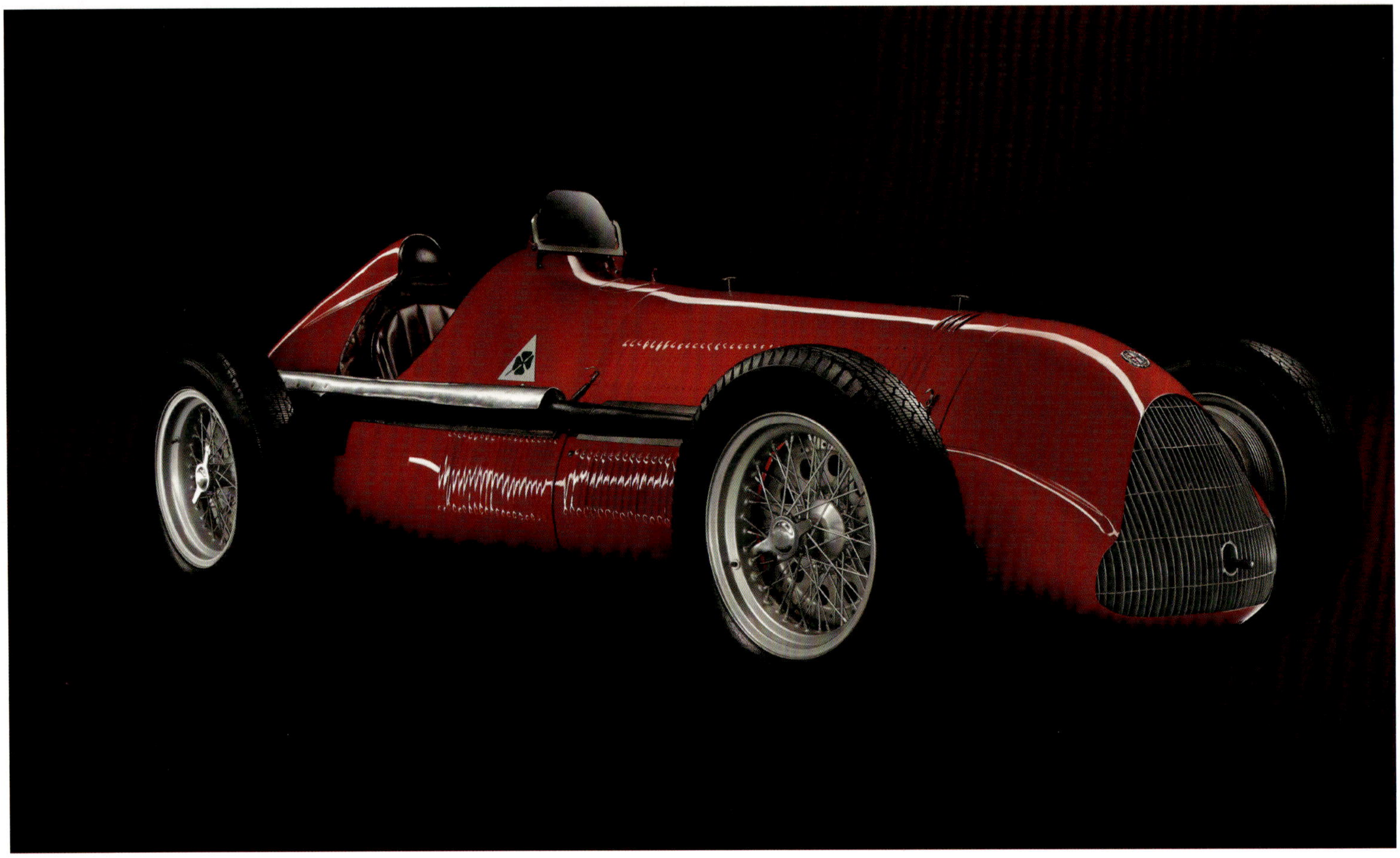

WORLD CHAMPION AGAIN!

In 1950, the most important Grand Prix races were combined to form the new Formula 1 World Championship. The first two titles went to Alfa Romeo factory drivers.

Because the *Tipo 158* looked almost dainty alongside previous Grand Prix cars, it was nicknamed *Alfetta*, or little Alfa. The steering wheel is almost vertical, and the gearshift lever is on the left.

***Following spread*: Driving the *Tipo 159*, which had been further developed for the 1951 season, Juan Manuel Fangio won the rainy Swiss Grand Prix in Bern. The Argentinean also became world champion that year.**

War. Newly developed cars, however, were the exception in those days, with the tense economic and raw materials situation. Alfa Romeo, a dominant brand in Grand Prix racing in the 1930s, relied on the Tipo 158, which had been developed as early as 1937. With a small 91.5-cubic-inch (1.5-liter) straight eight-cylinder engine, the model was designed for the *voiturette* category. Compared to the Alfa Romeo 308 or 312 Grand Prix cars with 3-liter engines, the almost tiny racer was nicknamed "*Alfetta*," or little Alfa.

The eight examples originally built had been hidden away during the war and were now being reactivated. The car's concept, which was already ten years old, was technically updated for its new beginning. The Tipo 158C's power was increased to 245 hp by adding a second supercharger. At the 1946 GP of Nations in Geneva (Switzerland), Italian driver Giuseppe "Nino" Farina celebrated the first postwar Grand Prix victory for Alfa Romeo.

Racing picked up again throughout Europe. For the 1950 season, the most important Grand Prix races were combined into a world championship for the first time since 1925. This consisted of seven races and was given a new name: Formula 1. Now, 91.5-cubic-inch (1.5-liter) engines with turbocharging were permitted—perfect for Alfa Romeo—or 275 cubic inches (4.5 liters) without turbocharging, tailor-made for Team Ferrari, which was founded in 1947.

Alfa Romeo sent a team into the race that would go down in history as the "Three Big Fs": Italian drivers Nino Farina and Luigi Fagioli and Argentinean Juan Manuel Fangio. Farina, who studied economics, was the nephew of Battista Farina, the founder of the later Pininfarina design studio. He had been driving for Alfa Romeo since 1933. Before the Second World War, Fagioli won for the factory teams of Maserati, Mercedes, and Auto Union but had to hang up his helmet for health reasons. Already forty-nine years old, he returned with Alfa Romeo after the end of the war. With victory at the 1951 French GP—where he shared the car with Fangio—he became the oldest Formula 1 winner of all time. Fangio came to Europe only in 1949, having mainly driven road races in Argentina. He won straight away for Maserati and switched to Alfa Romeo for the 1950 season. With a total of five titles, Fangio became the dominant driver in the early stages of Formula 1.

But let's not get ahead of ourselves. On May 13, 1950, the first race of the new Formula 1 World Championship took place at Silverstone in the UK. Alfa Romeo had once again improved the Tipo 158 for this purpose. With fine-tuning work on the superchargers and the intake tract, the engine's power output had risen to 350 hp—with a displacement of 1.5 liters as before.

Farina won the Formula 1 premiere in England. The Italian also won at Bremgarten (Switzerland) and Spa-Francorchamps (Belgium). Teammate Fangio also took

24

May 13, 1950, at Silverstone, England: Nino Farina (*below*) wins the European Grand Prix, the first Formula 1 race in history, driving the Alfa Romeo *Tipo 158*.

three victories, at Monaco, Reims (France), and Monza (Italy). In the end, Farina's better fourth result (fourth place in Belgium) determined that he would become the first Formula 1 World Champion in history ahead of his teammate Fangio.

After the end of the season, engine guru Gioacchino Colombo, the mastermind behind the Tipo 158 in 1937, returned to Alfa Romeo from Ferrari. Under his direction, the 1.5-liter eight-cylinder engine was revised once again. With new superchargers and methanol as fuel, it was now capable of 425 hp. So that the drivers did not have to refuel too often during the up-to-497-mile-long (800km) Grand Prix, the body was extended to the rear to accommodate an additional fuel tank. The chassis was also modernized. The 1951 Grand Prix racer was given the type designation 159.

The season was marked by the duel between the defending champion from Portello and the team of former Alfa Romeo racing director Enzo Ferrari. At the season opener in Silverstone, the Scuderia inflicted the first defeat on the Alfa Romeo factory team in a world championship race. In the course of the year, Alfa Romeo won four Grand Prix races—Fangio three times, Farina once—while Ferrari celebrated three victories. As in the previous year, both teams missed out on the US GP, the only Grand Prix outside Europe. So Juan-Manuel Fangio became world champion ahead of Ferrari driver Alberto Ascari.

Alfa Romeo succeeded in defending its title; nevertheless the brand withdrew from Grand Prix racing. The era of one of the most successful Formula 1 cars of all time was over. The Tipo 158/159 started in a total of fifty-three Grand Prix races, most of which were held outside the World Championship, as was customary at the time. The *Alfetta* crossed the finish line as the winner forty-seven times—a success rate of 89 percent.

THREE MAGIC LETTERS

In the 1960s, Alfa Romeo celebrated success on the racetrack with a model whose name still stands for inspiring technology today: GTA.

After withdrawing from Formula 1, Alfa Romeo concentrated on sports car racing. When a world championship was organized for this vehicle category in 1953, Alfa Romeo president Giuseppe Luraghi recognized a new field of activity for a factory team. Chief designer Giuseppe Busso was commissioned to develop a GT racing car.

Busso drew largely on the technology of the *Giulia* series of cars, which was about to be launched on the market. But instead of a self-supporting body as in the *Giulia*, he envisaged a tubular frame (Italian: *tubolare*) as the supporting structure for the racing car. Zagato, a guarantor of extreme lightweight construction since the 1930s, was responsible for the body design. Naturally, the body was made entirely of aluminum. This reduced the weight of the *Giulia Tubolare Zagato* (TZ) to less than 1,543 pounds (700 kg).

That left the engine. Alfa Romeo commissioned Carlo Chiti to build it. The aerospace engineer from Tuscany had previously designed racing cars for Alfa Romeo. At Ferrari, he developed, among other things, the Formula 1 world championship cars from 1958 and 1961. Chiti and some colleagues went into business for themselves in

The *Giulia GTA* (*opposite*) was not the only car developed by Autodelta for Alfa Romeo. From Udine and later Settimo Milanese also came the TZ (*top photo, front row center*), the Tipo 33/2 (*rear left*), the Tipo 33TT12 (*rear right*), and even Formula 1 racing cars.

Carlo Chiti is what one would now call a workaholic. The Alfa Romeo TZ had its origins in his idea. *Opposite*: The TZ2 in front of the doors of the Autodelta factory at Settimo Milanese.

1963 with the moderately successful ATS racing team. In order to fill Alfa Romeo's order, Chiti, together with business partner Lodovico Chizzola, founded Autodelta, a company that would play a major role in the Alfa Romeo racing team in the decades to come. For a while, Chiti worked at ATS in Bologna during the day and at Autodelta in Udine at night.

A 150hp racing version of the 97.6-cubic-inch (1.6-liter) engine from the *Giulia* was developed there. The one hundred or so Giulia TZs required for eligibility to compete in motor racing were also built there. In 1964 and 1965, Alfa Romeo contested the World Endurance Championship with the *Giulia TZ*. The factory drivers regularly won their class, including at the 24-hour race at Le Mans.

After two years of success, it was time to update the *Giulia TZ*. In October 1964, Autodelta unveiled its successor, the TZ2. The chassis remained unchanged except for a few minor modifications. The 1.6-liter engine was fitted with dual ignition and now produced almost 170 hp. The four-cylinder engine could be placed even lower in the chassis, thanks to a dry sump lubrication system and the resulting significantly flatter oil pan. Together with the body, which was now made of fiberglass, this resulted in a significantly lower center of gravity. The *Giulia TZ2* was also almost 110 pounds (50 kg) lighter than its predecessor.

In total, fewer than a dozen TZ2 chassis are built, and they were used successfully in sports car races. But Alfa Romeo's racing department had long since had other plans. Instead of competing with the Giulia TZ2 for success in the 1.6-liter class, the team wanted to compete for overall victories in the future. For this purpose, a so-called prototype had to be developed, which finally became reality as the *Tipo 33*.

Until then, Autodelta was devoting more attention to the European Touring Car Championship. Very expensive GT cars such as the *Giulia TZ*, built in small numbers, were not used there, but rather racing cars that were at least visually reminiscent of large-scale production models.

The fans could identify with them much better. Tens of thousands of fans made the pilgrimage to the 1,000-kilometer (621-mile) race on the Nürburgring-Nordschleife, the four-hour race at Monza, or the 24-hour race at Spa-Francorchamps, Belgium. The races held behind the "Iron Curtain" in Budapest (Hungary) and Belgrade (Yugoslavia) were also a great success. In the mid-1960s, the European Touring Car Championship, in which numerous manufacturers were involved, even eclipsed Formula 1, which was then dominated by British private teams.

For the European Championship, Autodelta built a special, road-legal qualification vehicle based on the *Giulia Sprint*

AUTODELTA

Tudor
39
Firestone

Left: The Alfa Romeo *Giulia TZ* in the banked turn at Monza, which today is no longer part of the racetrack. *Opposite*: With the *Giulia GTA Junior* (photo by Toine Hezemans), in 1972 Alfa Romeo again won the brand title in the European Touring Car Championship.

GT coupe named GTA, unveiled in February 1965 at the Amsterdam Motor Show. The suffix "A" in the type designation was for the Italian term *alleggerita* (lightened). The addition refers to the car's reduced curb weight compared to the conventional *Giulia Sprint GT*.

This was made possible by the use of Peraluman, a very light aluminum-zinc-manganese alloy, in the car's body. Only the floor panel and the roof pillars were still made of sheet steel. In addition, the interior was very spartan—the dashboard of some models consisted of little more than decorative foil. As a result, the GTA was around 440 pounds (200 kg) lighter than a conventional *Sprint GT*. Its 1.6-liter engine had dual ignition and two 45 Weber twin carburetors. Just under 170 hp was available in the factory tuned "*Corsa*" variant.

The GTA became the dominant vehicle in the 1.6-liter class of the European Touring Car Championship. Factory driver Andrea de Adamich (Italy) became European champion in this category in 1966 and 1967, and Spartaco Dini (Italy) was champion in 1969. Alfa Romeo also won the brand title in these years. In addition, the GTA carried private drivers to the European Mountain Championship and numerous national titles. Herbert Schultze, for example, became the German circuit champion with the GTA in 1968 and 1969.

At the end of 1969, the Autodelta racing department launched the GTA's big brother. Its name, GTAm (m for *maggiorata*), referred to the thick fender extensions and an increased engine displacement of 2 liters. With the GTAm, Dutchman Toine Hezemans won the European Drivers' Championship in 1970, and in 1971, Alfa Romeo won the brand title.

In 1972, Alfa Romeo was able to defend this title, but with the *GTA Junior*, with a 1.3-liter engine, the little brother of the 2-liter GTAm. Autodelta delivered the four-cylinder in the Corsa variant with up to 160 hp. This made the GTAm 1300 almost unbeatable in the small displacement class. Alfa Romeo drivers won the division in all nine TWEM races in 1972.

TRIUMPH AND TEARS

Alfa Romeo twice became world champion in endurance races in the 1970s. Its comeback in Formula 1, on the other hand, was not very successful.

Parallel to its successful involvement in the European Touring Car Championship, Alfa Romeo prepared its entry into the prototype class of the World Endurance Championship at the end of the 1960s. The series included such famous events as the "24 Hours of Le Mans," the 12-hour race at Sebring (USA), and the 1,000-kilometer race on the Nürburgring, but at times road races such as the *Mille Miglia* as well.

The Tipo 33, a two-seater mid-engine coupe, marked the beginning of Alfa Romeo's involvement. Autodelta developed a chassis, which in the road version received a breathtaking body by star designer Franco Scaglione. While the *Tipo 33 Stradale* had a closed cockpit, the racing department preferred a Spider. In both cases, the engine was a 2-liter V-8 with a 90-degree bank angle; 270 hp was specified for racing.

In the 1968 world championship, the *Tipo 33/2* regularly won the 2-liter class but still did not manage any overall victories. Autodelta therefore followed up with the *Tipo 33/3*, which had an eight-cylinder engine with 3 liters of displacement under the hood. And indeed—on April 4, 1971, Alfa Romeo won a race in the World Sports Car Championship for the first time. Henri Pescarolo (France) and Andrea de Adamich (Italy) won the 1,000-kilometer race at Brands Hatch (Great Britain) ahead of a factory Ferrari.

Left: Race director Carlo Chiti (*wearing coat*) next to the *Tipo 179* Formula 1 racing car with driver Mario Andretti in the cockpit. *Opposite*: With the *Tipo 33TT12* (here at the Nürburgring with Derek Bell at the wheel), Alfa Romeo won the World Championship for Makes in 1975.

In 1968, Alfa Romeo celebrated a triple victory by the *Tipo 33/2* in the 2-liter class at the "24 Hours of Le Mans." *Opposite*: Arturo Merzario (*in cowboy hat*) and team at the 1000-kilometer (621-mile) race at Zeltweg (Austria) in 1975.

For the 1972 season, Carlo Chiti revised the engine, which now produced 440 hp. The biggest change, however, was in the chassis. The new Tipo 33TT had a tubular frame (Italian: *Telaio Tubolare*, abbreviated TT) as its supporting structure. In 1973, Autodelta ignited the next stage—the eight-cylinder engine was replaced by a twelve-cylinder. The boxer engine officially produced 450 hp, but the competition suspected a few more. The first victory for the *Tipo 33TT12* in the world championship came in 1974, when Formula 1 drivers Mario Andretti (USA) and Arturo Merzario (Italy) won the 1,000-kilometer race at Monza (Italy) in the service of the Alfa Romeo factory team.

For the 1975 season, Alfa Romeo teamed up with the team of German entrepreneur Willi Kauhsen. While Autodelta prepared the *Tipo 33TT12*, the WKRT team was responsible for the races. This cooperation worked perfectly. With seven victories in eight starts, Alfa Romeo became world champion.

Two years later, another title went to Alfa Romeo. The racing car in the 1977 season was still the *Tipo 33*, but now with a monocoque instead of a tubular frame as the supporting structure. The model designation was therefore changed to 33SC12, with SC standing for the Italian term for monocoque (*scatolato*). The twelve-cylinder boxer engine now produced 510 hp.

In 1977, the World Championship of Makes consisted of a total of seventeen races. Eight prototypes, officially named Group 6 sports cars, such as the *Tipo 33SC12*, competed in eight of these. The Alfa Romeo works drivers won all eight races. Alfa Romeo was thus crowned sports car world champion.

The main contributor to both world championship titles was Arturo Merzario, with a total of four victories. The Italian driver became European Hillclimb champion in 1969 before making his debut in Formula 1 with Ferrari in 1972. At that time, it was common practice for Grand Prix drivers to also compete in other racing series. Thus Merzario, who always appeared in a cowboy hat because of a cigarette sponsor, drove for Williams in Formula 1 and at the same time for Alfa Romeo in endurance races. In 1976, he became world famous when he pulled Niki Lauda out of his burning Ferrari on the Nürburgring, saving his life. At the end of his active career, Arturo Merzario became an ambassador for the Alfa Romeo brand.

However, Merzario was not on board when Alfa Romeo returned to Formula 1 in 1979. At that time, Autodelta had already been supplying the Brabham team with the twelve-cylinder engines of the *Tipo 33* for three years. Niki Lauda won two Grand Prix races in the Brabham-Alfa Romeo. On May 13, 1979, the time had come—at the Belgian Grand Prix, Alfa Romeo returned to Formula 1 with its own team. The racer called the *Tipo 177* was still powered by the twelve-cylinder engine with a 180-degree bank angle. But with such a flat but wide engine, the latest trend in the

MARTHA"
CAMPARI
GOODYEAR
Agip
GOODYEAR
GOODYEAR
A. MERZARIO
Marlboro

12
LOCKHEED

Preceding pages: The Alfa Romeo *Tipo 33-3* during the 1,000-kilometer (621-mile) race on the Nürburgring in 1971, here with Nino Varracella at the wheel. *Right*: A look inside Autodelta's workshop: in the foreground mechanics are working on a *Tipo 33TT12*, while behind it is an *Alfetta GTV*, and in the far rear an *Alfasud*.

Right: Alfa Romeo returned to Formula 1 racing in 1979 with the *Tipo 177*.

WITH A CYLINDER BANK ANGLE OF 180 DEGREES, THE TIPO 33'S TWELVE-CYLINDER ENGINE WAS UNIQUE IN ITS CLASS.

chassis sector, the so-called wing car, which generated a lot of downforce, was not feasible. Autodelta has therefore long been working on a V-12 engine with a 60-degree bank angle. It celebrated its premiere in the *Tipo 179* at the Italian GP in autumn 1979. This Grand Prix was also the last race for the Brabham-Alfa Romeo—the previous partners went their separate ways from then on.

For four years, Alfa Romeo used the *Tipo 179*, which was constantly being improved, but with moderate success. By then, a completely new car was needed. The reason was a revolution in the engine sector. Since 1977, engines with turbocharging have been used in Formula 1 alongside conventional naturally aspirated engines. Although they were subject to a displacement handicap—a maximum of 1.5 liters instead of the 3.0 liters for naturally aspirated engines—the turbos consistently outstripped the naturally aspirated engines.

Autodelta therefore designed a V-8 turbo engine, which made its debut in 1982 in the *Tipo 182T* at the home Grand Prix in Monza. In the 1983 season, Alfa Romeo cooperated with the Euroracing team. Relatively modest results led to heated discussions between motor racing supplier Autodelta, still headed by Carlo Chiti, and the Euroracing design department. Even the newly designed Alfa Romeo 184T for the 1984 season did not bring the hoped-for turnaround—it was conspicuous mainly for its brightly colored livery in the colors of the principal sponsor Benetton. At the end of the 1985 season, Alfa Romeo withdrew from Formula 1 for the second time.

***Above*: Alfa Romeo returned to Formula 1 racing in 1979 with the *Tipo 177*. *Following pages*: In the 1984 Formula 1 season, the Alfa Romeo 184T was driven by the American Eddie Cheever (*in photo*) and Riccardo Patrese from Italy.**

Agip

SISLEY
GOODYEAR
CHAMPION
012
TURBO
LARGEST KNITWEAR PRODUCER
23
FERODO
arexons

REPEAT OFFENDER

In the 1980s, Alfa Romeo again became European Touring Car Champion. The close relationship between the road car and the racing car is interesting.

For the 1982 season, new regulations came into force in the European Touring Car Championship. In the so-called Group A, large-series cars (at least 5,000 built per year) were required effective immediately, with only limited improvements. These near-series regulations were entirely to Alfa Romeo's liking.

Autodelta was developing a racing version of the GTV6, whose 2.5-liter six-cylinder engine was tuned to around 215 hp (156 hp in production cars). The biggest advantage of the Italian wedge, however, was its optimal weight distribution between its front and rear axles. This was made possible by the unique transaxle concept—the gearbox and clutch were combined into one block with the rear axle differential. This enabled the Alfa GTV6 to transfer the driving force more effectively to the road surface.

At the beginning of the 1980s, about a dozen endurance races were held in the European Championship, including the season's highlight, the "24 Hours of Spa-Francorchamps" in Belgium. Between 1982 and 1986, the GTV6 won more than forty races in the displacement class up to 2.5 liters. Thanks to these successes, Alfa Romeo won the manufacturers' title in the European championship four times in a row. The GTV6 also celebrated successes in national championships, including the German Production Car Championship (DTM) with former world-class skier Franz Klammer.

Opposite: Alfa Romeo competed in the 1987 World Touring Car Championship with the 75 Turbo. The drivers were Paolo Barilla, Jean-Louis Schlesser, Michael Andretti, and Alessandro Nannini (*above*). *Below*: Two Alfa Romeo GTV6s competed in the 1984 German Touring Car Championship.

In 1987, the European Touring Car Championship was upgraded to a World Championship. Alfa Romeo competed with the successor to the GTV6, the *75 Turbo*. The racing car was based on the special model *75 Turbo Evoluzione*, of which just 500 were made. The racing department modified the standard car with wide flared fenders, a large front spoiler, a rear spoiler lip, and a multi-adjustable suspension. The 1.8-liter turbo engine produced 280 hp in racing trim (standard production version: 155 hp).

Seven of the eleven world championship races, each covering 310 miles (500 km) with a driver change, took place in Europe, the rest in Australia, New Zealand, and Japan. There were constant disputes about the interpretation of the technical regulations, including subsequent disqualifications. As a result, the championship was abolished after just one year.

Alfa Romeo concentrated on the Italian championship with the further developed *75 Turbo*. In 1988, private driver Gianfranco Brancatelli became champion. From 1990 onward, the regulations gave the engineers more freedom. As a result, the power of the *75 Turbo* rose to 400 hp. In 1992, the *Tipo 155 GTA* replaced the *75 Turbo*.

The *Giro d'Italia* is a mixture of circuit and rally, covering almost 1,243 miles (2,000 km) across Italy. For this race, in which two drivers—plus a co-driver for the rally stages—share a car, Alfa Romeo built two very special *75 Turbos* with well over 400 hp. Even wider mudguards allowed wheels with a width of 11 inches, and all hoods and the windows were made of plastic. A huge rear spoiler provided tremendous downforce on the rear axle.

The car was not only visually and acoustically stunning, it was also fast: in 1988, Formula 1 driver Riccardo Patrese, who drove the circuits, and the rally duo of Miki Biasion and Tiziano Siviero won the *Giro d'Italia*. In 1989, the combination of Giorgio Francia (circuit) and Dario Cerrato and Giuseppe Cerri emerged victorious.

Lella Lombardi and Giorgio Francia won their displacement class in the Alfa Romeo GTV6 at the 24-hour race at Spa-Francorchamps.

ARTOIS LIGHT
Mobil
smet jet
UNIROYAL
SECA
motor show
AUTOBERGAMO
41
PIRELLI P7

Larini
Philips Car Systems
DEKRA
8
BÄUMLER
men's fashion
BÄUMLER
men's fashion
MICHELIN
speedline
MICHELIN
ERG

AMONG SHARKS

Alfa Romeo ventured into the DTM, which was dominated by German manufacturers—with the most technically complex touring car ever.

At the end of the 1980s, the German Touring Car Championship (DTM) developed into the most important championship for racing cars based on production sedans. Alfa Romeo was the only foreign manufacturer to challenge the strong domestic brands.

In 1993, the so-called Class 1 regulations were introduced in the DTM, giving the engineers a great deal of freedom. Alfa Romeo developed a Class 1 racer based on the 155 model, with a body that largely corresponded to the standard version. But below an imaginary line through the two wheel hubs, the aerodynamicists had a lot of freedom. The same applied to the engine. Limits were set primarily by the maximum permissible engine capacity of 2.5 liters. There was also a free choice of powertrain.

Alfa Romeo opted for all-wheel drive. The V-6 sat very low and far behind the front axle. At the beginning of the season, 420 hp was mentioned as the power output. The six-cylinder engine reached up to 12,000 rpm, which is almost Formula 1 territory. The body of the *155 V6 TI* was largely made of carbon fiber.

The Italian Alfa Romeo factory drivers Nicola Larini and Alessandro Nannini, both with Formula 1 experience, immediately felt at home in the shark tank that is the DTM. They won twelve of a total of 20 races in the 1993 season.

Shock for the home team—newcomer Alfa Romeo and its 155 V6 TI won the German Touring Car Championship (DTM) in 1993, while Nicola Larini emerged as the drivers' champion. *Following pages*: The 1995 version of the Alfa Romeo 155 V6 TI was even lower.

MARTINI
8
Agip
MICHELIN

MANN
Larini
DEKRA
8
MARTINI
OZ
MAGNETI MARELLI
UMLER
momo

A look under the carbon fiber body of the Alfa Romeo 155 V6 TI: the V-6 engine sits extremely low and distributes its output to all four wheels.

Alfa Romeo competed in the European and World Touring Car Championships from 2001 to 2007 with the *Superturismo* version of the 156.

Alfa Romeo thus won the manufacturers' title–which came as a shock to the German competition.

Larini, who was eventually celebrated as champion, singlehandedly achieved ten victories. Born in Tuscany, he took the classic route via junior formulae to Formula 1. After forty-nine Grand Prix races, including some for Ferrari, he switched to the Alfa Romeo factory touring car team. With the title of Italian champion in his pocket in 1992, Larini shook up the DTM a year later. He won both races on the Nürburgring-Nordschleife, a feat that was considered practically impossible for Nordschleife newcomers until then.

In the following three years, Alfa Romeo continued to win in the DTM and the International Touring Car Championship (ITC), which transferred the DTM concept to a worldwide racing series. During this time, the 155 V6 TI underwent constant development. Advances included an ABS system that also worked with all-wheel drive, hydraulics for aerodynamically favorable lowering of the body, flaps for the air intakes in the front that moved for the same reason, and a fully automatic gearbox. The competitors noticed this only because the onboard cameras showed that the Alfa Romeo drivers were not changing gears themselves. In 1996, the 2.5-liter naturally aspirated V-6 engine of the Alfa Romeo 155 V6 TI produced almost 500 hp.

Class 1 produced the most fascinating touring cars of all time. However, at some point the ever-escalating technology race was no longer affordable. At the end of 1996, the bubble burst, and the DTM and ITC were discontinued. The Alfa Romeo 155 V6 TI and all its competitors were consigned to museums.

As a new field of activity, Alfa Romeo chose the European Super Touring Cup, which was given the status of a European championship from 2001. Here, the technical freedoms were considerably less; the cubic capacity limit for the naturally aspirated engines was 2 liters. Alfa Romeo opted for the 156 model, which was new at the time, as its basic car.

The body remained almost standard. Only the rear spoiler, which was standard for all vehicles, and the front spoiler, which was designed to be more aerodynamically efficient within the scope of the standard dimensions, bore witness to the motorsport genes of the Milanese racing sedan. The four-valve engine produced around 305 hp at the rev limit of 8,500 rpm.

Alfa Romeo works driver Fabrizio Giovanardi won the European Super Touring Cup in 2000, and the European Championship, which was announced as the "FIA European Super Touring Championship," one year later. For 2002, the touring car regulations were revised, combined with

The cars that take part in the WTCR (World Touring Car Cup) series must be production models, which enhance its popularity. The Alfa Romeo *Giulietta* began competing in this series of races in 2018. The car was developed by a private Italian team.

a renewed renaming of the championship as the FIA European Touring Car Championship (ETCC). Alfa Romeo had to modify the 156 GTA accordingly. In some areas (e.g., front spoiler, wing extensions), there was now greater freedom; in others (e.g., engine, brakes, gearbox), the engineers had to retrofit.

The further-developed Alfa Romeo 156 also remained the dominant car in the ETCC. With thirteen of twenty possible victories, the manufacturers' title went to Milan in 2002, and Giovanardi became drivers' champion. One year later, newcomer Gabriele Tarquini won the third European title in a row for Alfa Romeo.

In 2005, the European Championship was promoted to the World Championship; the ETCC became the WTCC (FIA World Touring Car Championship). From 2006, Alfa Romeo was represented there by the private team N. Technology. Under the direction of N.Technology, the Alfa Romeo drivers celebrated several more victories before the racing career of the 156 model finally came to an end at the conclusion of the 2007 season.

After that, Alfa Romeo was no longer involved in touring car racing. However, private teams continued to represent the brand's colors. For example, Romeo Ferraris were active in the worldwide WTCR series (World Touring Car Racing) with the *Giulietta* from 2018. The small team from the south of Milan has won a number of races with the 330 hp near-series racer.

YOKOHAMA
K. Ceccon
31
abmedica
MOTUL
MOTUL
KW
YOKOHAMA
KW
YOKOHAMA

68
Alfa Romeo
68

STILL RACING

The historic Alfa Romeo racing cars are much too beautiful to sit in the factory museum with flat tires.

Museum vehicles often smell musty. Many of the vehicles exhibited in the *Museo Storico Alfa Romeo* in Arese exude a slight smell of burned petrol, hot brakes, and tire wear. The reason: they are not in a state of permanent sleep but are regularly brought out from the hallowed halls of the factory museum and used in historic racing events.

The specially formed *Automobilismo Storico Alfa Romeo* (Alfa Romeo Historic Automobiles) department competes at highlights such as the *Mille Miglia Storico* and the *Gran Premio Nuvolari* in Italy, the "Goodwood Festival of Speed" in England, and the Schloss Dyck Classic Days in Germany. The cars range from the Tipo 6C 1500 *Sport Speciale* from the 1930s to the *Tipo 2000 Sportiva* from 1954 and the 1993 DTM winner, the Alfa Romeo 155 V6 TI. Often the entries are run by Scuderia Portello, a private team from north of Milan named after Alfa Romeo's first headquarters.

The activities of *Automobilismo Storico Alfa Romeo* have a clear objective: to promote the image of the brand and to make car fans feel the great tradition of Alfa Romeo. For this reason, the museum's historic racing cars are often driven by prominent contemporaries, who also attract the attention of the media. The second strategy is to invite the best specialists for classic car racing to take the wheel in order to shine with sporting successes.

This tactic works. The historic Alfa Romeo works team has already celebrated several overall victories at the *Mille Miglia Storico*, the most renowned and most difficult classic car event in the world. This proves that the *cuore sportivo* (sporting heart) beats with undiminished power even in Alfa Romeo cars that are more than half a century old.

Only vehicles that started in the original races between 1927 and 1957 are eligible to take part in the *Mille Miglia Storico* vintage rally. The Alfa Romeo 6C 1750 is still winning on the route from Brescia to Rome and back.

Svizzera
7
MAGNETI MARELLI
axitea
PIRELLI
SINGHA
CARRERA

COMEBACK WITH EISMANN

After a three-decade pause, Alfa Romeo returned to Formula 1 in 2018. One season later, a former world champion joined its cadre of drivers.

The location of the presentation was carefully chosen—shortly before Christmas 2017, the Alfa Romeo Sauber F1 Team introduced itself to the public in the magnificent factory museum in Arese. The brand-new car bearing the Alfa Romeo logo was to be flanked by legendary Grand Prix and Formula 1 racers from the brand's history. "Alfa Romeo is now back where the brand belongs," said Sergio Marchionne, President of Fiat Chrysler Automobiles (FCA) and responsible for Alfa Romeo, welcoming the 500 journalists and guests of honor.

After a break of three decades, Alfa Romeo was returning to Formula 1 for the 2018 season as the title sponsor of Team Sauber. The traditional Swiss team employed around 400 people at its Hinwil site near Zurich. Sauber designed and manufactured most of the 7,000 or so individual parts that made up the Formula 1 racer's chassis. Around one hundred technicians alone were employed in the aerodynamics department. In the company's own wind tunnel, one of the best in the world, new front spoilers or rear wings could be tested around the clock if necessary. Just a stone's throw away, about eighty designers in a huge open-plan office were working on ways to make the Formula 1 cars with the Alfa Romeo logo on the hood even faster. Through a window, one could see the assembly hall, where up to six racing cars were being worked on at the same time under practically clinically clean conditions.

Finnish driver Kimi Räikkönen celebrates his Formula 1 debut in 2001 with the Swiss racing team Sauber. The "Iceman," as he is known because of his cool headedness, returned to Sauber, Alfa Romeo's partner in Grand Prix sport, for the 2019 season.

The engine, a V-6 turbo engine with a capacity of 1.6 liters, was supplied to the team by Ferrari. The regulations stipulated a rev limit (15,000 rpm), which was intended to improve durability and thus reduce costs. The limitation of the flow rate in the fuel supply system, which was also prescribed, limited the conventionally generated power of the engine to about 700 hp. Two additional electric motors gave the Formula 1 engines a system output of over 900 hp.

The electricity required for propulsion was generated in two different ways. First, the kinetic energy released during braking was converted into electrical energy by the MGU-K (Motor Generator Unit Kinetic). Second, the turbocharger drove a second generator via a shaft, which also fed the battery. The MGU-H (Motor Generator Unit Heat) was also used to improve the response of the turbocharger during acceleration. This hybrid technology made the Formula 1 engines the most efficient power units in the history of the racing series. The minimum weight of the entire vehicle prescribed by the regulations was 1,631 pounds (740 kg).

In the inaugural year of 2018, Swede Marcus Ericsson and Frenchman Charles Leclerc, Formula 2 champion and member of the Ferrari junior squad, were chosen to drive the Alfa Romeo C37, as the racer was called in the old Sauber tradition. At the end of the season, the Alfa Romeo Sauber F1 Team was eighth in the constructors' championship.

Beginning with the 2019 season, the official team name would be Alfa Romeo Racing, with the important addition of "since 1910" as a reference to the brand's more than hundred-year history. A spectacular new signing caused even more of a stir: Kimi Räikkönen, Formula 1 World Champion in 2007.

Strictly speaking, Räikkönen was making a comeback at Sauber. Born in Espoo in southern Finland, he rose through the junior ranks until Peter Sauber brought him into his Formula 1 team in 2001. Just one year later, Räikkönen switched to McLaren and celebrated his first Grand Prix victory. Journalists despaired of the taciturn Finn. He drove entire press conferences to despair by answering questions with a taciturn "Yes," "No," or "I don't know." Or he snapped at his race engineer over the radio, "Leave me alone; I know what I'm doing." Ron Dennis, his former team boss at McLaren, once jokingly called Räikkönen "Iceman." The name stuck.

In 2007, he was hired by Ferrari as Michael Schumacher's successor. The "Iceman" became world champion on his first attempt but was unable to build on this success in the years that followed. The Scuderia released him for 2010–with full salary.

In addition to regular driver Kimi Räikkönen (*top photo*), Alfa Romeo Racing employed the Colombian Tatiana Calderon (*bottom photo*) as a test driver. The team traveled to the Formula 1 races with around seventy-five people. *Following pages*: The choreography of the pit stops, in which all four tires are changed in less than four seconds, is practiced countless times.

DHL
STROLL
Svizzera
RICHARD MILLE
Alfa Romeo

ALFA ROMEO HAS COME FULL CIRCLE. AFTER WINNING THE 1950 AND 1951 TITLES, THE BRAND IS BACK IN THE ROYAL CLASS OF FORMULA 1.

Rain dance—in the 2018 debut season, Charles Leclerc, who later became a Ferrari driver, drove the Alfa Romeo C37.

After two years in the World Rally Championship, Räikkönen returned to Formula 1 in 2012 for Lotus, rejoined Ferrari in 2014, and switched to Alfa Romeo Racing in 2019. His teammate was the Italian Antonio Giovinazzi. Their Alfa Romeo Racing C38s were not only technically an evolution of the 2018 C37s. They also got a paint job specially developed by Centro Stile Alfa Romeo. A nice detail: Kimi Räikkönen's racer (starting number 7) bore the *Stelvio* logo on the air scoop, while teammate Antonio Giovinazzi (number 99) drove a *Giulia*. The team finished the 2019 season once again in eighth place in the constructors' championship.

The following year, the Pole Robert Kubica came on board as a new test driver to support Räikkönen and Giovinazzi. The official team name was changed to Alfa Romeo Racing ORLEN in deference to their personal sponsor, a petroleum company. A minor sensation was the signing of the second development driver. With the Colombian Tatiana Calderón, a woman had joined the exclusive circle of Formula 1 drivers for the first time in a long time.

***Following pages*: 2020 automobiles in historic colors—the Alfa Romeo *Stelvio* wears Verde Visconti (Visconti green), while the Alfa Romeo *Giulia* is painted Rosso Competizione (competition red).**

Schweiz
16
CARRERA
Claro

GB 139AY

FZ-237PP

1600 Junior Z 1972